DK GARDENING

SHRUBS & CLIMBERS

RICHARD ROSENFELD

A DORLING KINDERSLEY BOOK

LONDON, NEW YORK,
MUNICH, MELBOURNE, DELHI

Series Editor Zia Allaway
Series Art Editor Alison Donovan
Managing Editor Anna Kruger
Managing Art Editor Lee Griffiths
Consultant Louise Abbott
DTP Designer Louise Waller
Media Resources Richard Dabb, Lucy Claxton
Picture Research Bridget Tily
Production Controller Mandy Inness

Produced on behalf of Dorling Kindersley by
HILTON/SADLER
Editorial director: Jonathan Hilton
Design director: Peggy Sadler

Introduction Text Zia Allaway

First published in Great Britain in 2003 by
Dorling Kindersley Limited
80 Strand, London, WC2R ORL
A Penguin company

Copyright © 2003
Dorling Kindersley Limited, London

A CIP catalogue record for this book is available
from The British Library
ISBN 0 7513 3820 6

Colour reproduction by Colourscan, Singapore
Printed and bound by Printer Trento, Italy

see our complete catalogue at
www.dk.com

Gardening with shrubs and climbers

FOR YEAR-ROUND INTEREST in the garden you can't beat shrubs and climbers. These essential plants provide permanent structure and add height, while also offering flowers, foliage and fragrance into the bargain. A carefully considered selection will ensure a continuous performance month after month, with catkins and blossom in spring, flowers throughout the summer, berries and bright foliage in autumn, and a finale in winter of colourful bark, frosted stems and vivid evergreens.

Whether creating a new border or planning a whole garden, it's best to plant your shrubs and climbers before flowering perennials and annuals, which can be used to fill in the gaps. Choose plants carefully, and ensure that they suit the site, soil and space available in your garden. Look carefully at the heights and spreads of your selection, and don't be fooled by the size of plants on sale at garden centres and nurseries, as these are often immature and will grow quickly once planted.

Take note, too, of the seasons in which the plants flower or fruit, so that you can enjoy an evolving display. Foliage is another important consideration, because it has the most enduring effect.

◀ **Tiny fragrant shrubs**, such as thyme, can be squeezed into paving cracks and small pots.

▶ **Bold variegated foliage** offers colour over a long period, unlike transient flowers.

Using shrubs and climbers

Shrubs and climbers have many uses in gardens large and small, and even a tiny balcony or windowbox will provide space for a small shrub or two. These beautiful plants can be used to take centre stage, or to form a backdrop for colourful perennials and annuals. They can also help to evoke an atmosphere or create a garden

Easy-care shrub borders set against pale gravel are perfect for a low-maintenance garden.

style. A spiky yucca, for example, will immediately set the scene for an exotic theme, while lavender-edged paths and bay trees will help to define a Mediterranean-style garden.

If you want a low-maintenance garden, make use of easy-care shrubs. Once established, they will swamp

Frosted stems create a magical winter wonderland

weeds in summer, and many require just a light prune every year or two. Combine plants with different colours and textures in raised beds on a patio or in borders set into gravel to create a

long-lasting tapestry effect that will require very little looking after.

Hedges and edges

Shrubs suitable for hedging, such as laurel (*Prunus laurocerasus*), create natural boundaries around a garden, while a thorny hedge of

Roses and clematis are a match made in heaven, combining colourful flowers with sweet fragrance.

pyracantha has the added benefit of deterring intruders. More compact plants, such as box (*Buxus*) or lavender, also make excellent edging for paths and walkways.

Climbing high

People with small gardens are often frightened to use tall plants, worried that they will cast too much shade and take up valuable space. If this is a concern for you consider climbers, which add an important vertical dimension to a garden without taking up too much room, and can be used like wallpaper to decorate fences, walls, sheds and eyesores. Alternatively, use them to clamber up trees or through large shrubs.

Pots and patios

Containers planted with shrubs provide an architectural framework for patio displays, and work particularly well as a backdrop to potted flowers. Even big shrubs, such as viburnums, can survive happily in large containers when fed and watered regularly, while small shrubs are useful in windowboxes and baskets, where they make perfect companions for seasonal bedding. Pots filled with ericaceous compost also allow you to grow acid-loving azaleas and other lime haters in a garden with alkaline soil.

Pots of small hebes offer year-round foliage interest and can be used to set off more seasonal containers.

Clothe trellises and arches with leafy climbers to frame a vista punctuated by an urn or sculpture.

Some climbers also do well in large containers. Try the scented, slightly tender, star jasmine in a pot close to the back door for a spray of sweet perfume as you step outside. The plant can then be easily moved indoors for the winter.

Choosing shrubs and climbers

WHETHER YOU BUY your shrubs and climbers from a garden centre, nursery or supermarket, take care to select healthy plants that will get off to a good start when planted. Check the care label to ensure that those you plan to buy will suit the site and soil in your garden, as they will soon show signs of stress and may die if grown in the wrong conditions.

Well-balanced, even top-growth

Healthy, vigorous foliage, free from damage and disease

Well-developed, even framework of stems

Moist soil, free from weed growth

Choosing a healthy plant
When buying any plant, reject those that are wilted or have discoloured leaves. Ensure no roots are growing out of the bottom of the pot and tip the plant out to check that it has a well-developed, healthy root system.

Well-established root system with white root tips. The roots shouldn't be wrapped tightly around the edge

Planting a shrub

Pot-grown shrubs can be planted at any time of the year, but ensure that the ground is neither waterlogged nor frozen. Most plants like moist but free-draining soil, but if yours is heavy clay that's prone to waterlogging, increase the drainage by digging in horticultural grit – a barrowful per 1 sq m (3 sq ft) should do the trick. Free-draining soil can be improved by incorporating well-rotted compost. Water your shrub about an hour before you begin planting.

1 Digging the hole
After improving the soil (see above), choose a fine day to plant your shrub. You will need to dig a hole about twice the width and a little deeper than the rootball.

2 Adding organic matter
Mix the removed soil with organic matter and fork over the base and sides of the hole to loosen the earth. Water the hole and allow the moisture to drain away.

3 Checking the correct depth
Gently ease the shrub out of its container and position it in the hole. Use a cane to check that the plant is at the same depth as it was in its original pot.

4 Finishing off
Backfill around the shrub with the mixed soil and organic matter, firming gently with your heel or hands as you go. Apply a mulch, such as cocoa shells, over the soil.

Planting a climber against a wall

Choosing the right site and soil is as important for climbers as it is for shrubs, but you must also ensure that the plant has adequate support. Check the climber's maximum height for an idea of the size and type of support it requires.

Climbers that cling with tendrils will also need wires or other plants to twine around. When planting, remember that the soil in front of a wall or fence is very dry, and climbers should be sited at least 45cm (18in) away from them.

1 Preparing the site
Prepare the soil as for a shrub, and then dig a hole, 45cm (18in) from the wall, twice as wide and deeper than the rootball. Add well-rotted compost to the hole.

2 Aligning the climber
Water the climber an hour before planting. Then, water the hole, let it drain, and place the plant at a 45° angle. Use a cane to check the plant is at the right depth.

3 Tying up
Fill in as you would a shrub, then select four or five strong shoots, and tie in each one to a stake. Attach the stakes to the lowest horizontal wires on the wall.

4 Finishing off
Cut back any weak, damaged or wayward shoots, and then cover the surrounding soil with a deep mulch, keeping clear the area immediately around the stems.

Looking after shrubs and climbers

FOR THE BEST RESULTS, shrubs and climbers need a little looking after. A suitable site and soil are of primary importance, but watering, feeding and pruning are also crucial. Water young plants thoroughly when the top soil feels dry, rather than watering little and often which encourages roots to rise to the surface where they quickly dry out. You will need to water less frequently as plants mature and the roots can reach moisture at lower levels.

▲ Watering shrubs

A seep hose placed around the root area of establishing shrubs ensures that they get a thorough soaking, while reducing wastage through evaporation. The hose can be disguised with a decorative mulch.

◄ Feeding shrubs

Most shrubs and climbers benefit from an annual spring feed with a slow-release fertilizer applied over the root area. Follow the application rates on the packet carefully.

Windbreaks ►

Protect young or slightly tender plants in exposed sites with a windbreak. A fence with gaps between the panels or a hedge are ideal, as they reduce the force of the wind but allow some air to pass through, which prevents turbulence behind them.

Essential pruning tips

Pruning stimulates growth and promotes new shoots and buds. Prune out dead and diseased stems first, and cut back weak growth hard and strong growth lightly. Using sharp tools, make clean, well-placed cuts (see right) that will heal quickly and reduce the chance of diseases entering.

Opposite shoots
Cut straight across these stems just above a pair of buds or shoots.

Alternate shoots
Cut at 45°, just above the shoot, so that the lower cut is behind the bud.

Angled cut
Plants with alternate buds are pruned so that water doesn't collect on the bud.

Pruning after planting

Many deciduous shrubs respond well to being pruned just after planting. Pruning encourages more strong, healthy stems to develop and also helps to make the plant bushier. Always make your cuts just above an outward-facing bud, as this will develop into a stem that points away from the centre, reducing the likelihood of crossing and congested growth. Remember that if you prune stems back hard just before a plant flowers, you will lose the blooms for that year.

1 Removing dead wood
It is important to remove any dead, weak and spindly stems by cutting them right back to the base. This encourages new shoots to grow.

2 Easing congestion
Stems that touch may create wounds that leave the plant open to disease. Prune them back to an outward-facing bud or to the ground.

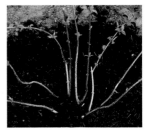

3 Creating balance
Lastly, cut out stems growing at an awkward angle that spoil the shape of the plant. Try to create an evenly branching, open framework.

Pruning a climber

The same principles apply to pruning climbers as to shrubs. Some climbers, such as jasmine (see below), have a permanent framework that can be pruned in late winter or early spring to keep them in shape. Others, with more lax growth, such as late-flowering clematis, should be cut back hard in the spring. New, vigorous stems will then shoot up from the base.

1 Removing crossing stems
Prune shoots that cross or touch with sharp secateurs. Cut back the wayward stems to healthy buds that are pointing in the direction you want them to grow.

2 Encouraging healthy, vigorous growth
Promote new, strong growth by pruning sideshoots back to a healthy, suitably placed bud. This can also stimulate the production of more flowering stems.

3 Removing the competition
Crowded stems at the centre of a plant will limit the air and light reaching the leaves, which can increase the likelihood of disease taking hold, and stunt growth.

4 Providing support
Use soft twine or plastic plant ties to tie in sideshoots securely to wires or trellis fixed to the support. Check the ties regularly and loosen as the stems thicken.

A-Z of Shrubs and Climbers

TAKING CUTTINGS

To create new plants for the garden, take semi-ripe cuttings at any time from early to late summer. The cuttings will readily root in a heated propagator.

A · *Abelia schumannii*

ARCHING STEMS WITH A LATE SEASON SHOW of 2.5cm (1in) long, gently scented, lilac-pink flowers make this a very useful shrub. The pinkish-green outer cases, or calyces, of the flowers hang on after the blooms have dropped. To thrive, abelias need a warm, sunny position and shelter from cold winds. Prune in the spring for shape, if necessary, and to thin out old wood to prompt new growth. An excellent alternative is *Abelia* x *grandiflora* 'Francis Mason' which is slightly smaller, and has yellow variegated leaves and coppery shoots.

OTHER VARIETIES *A.* 'Edward Goucher' (glossy dark green leaves, bronze when young); *A. floribunda* (taller-growing, bright cerise flowers); *A.* x *grandiflora* (pink-tinged white flowers).

PLANT PROFILE

HEIGHT 2m (6ft)

SPREAD 3m (10ft)

SITE Full sun

SOIL Fertile, free-draining

HARDINESS Frost hardy

FLOWERING Late summer to autumn

Abeliophyllum distichum White forsythia

A

WITH VANILLA-SCENTED FLOWERS opening from pink buds on bare, leafless stems, this is an indispensable plant for the late winter to early spring garden. To encourage abundant flowering, grow this shrub against a sunny, sheltered wall in free-draining soil. The best time to prune is immediately after flowering has finished, which encourages plenty of the new growth that will bear next year's flowers. If you have not seen this plant before, it really does resemble a white-flowering forsythia with a pink tinge to the petals.

OTHER VARIETY *A. distichum* Roseum Group (scented, deeper pink spring flowers).

PLANT PROFILE
HEIGHT 1.5m (5ft) or more
SPREAD 1.5m (5ft)
SITE Full sun
SOIL Free-draining
HARDINESS Fully hardy
FLOWERING Late winter or early spring

A

Abutilon megapotamicum Flowering maple

DANGLING, FLASHY, COLOURFUL FLOWERS (the red part is actually the flower's outer casing) make this one of the most striking of the flowering maples. The arching, evergreen or semi-evergreen twiggy stems look best when arranged against a sunny, sheltered wall, or in a richly coloured border. Being a native of Brazil, cold, wet winters are fatal, so either provide free-draining soil and a protective winter mulch of compost, or pot it up in the autumn and keep the plant in a bright, airy, frost-free place until the spring.

OTHER VARIETIES *A.* 'Ashford Red' (red flowers); *A.* 'Canary Bird' (yellow flowers); *A.* 'Kentish Belle' (apricot-yellow flowers with purple stamens); *A. pictum* 'Thompsonii' (orange-flushed salmon-pink flowers).

PLANT PROFILE
HEIGHT 2m (6ft)
SPREAD 2m (6ft)
SITE Full sun
SOIL Free-draining
HARDINESS Frost hardy
FLOWERING Summer to autumn

Acca sellowiana Pineapple guava

A

DON'T BE PUT OFF by this South American plant's exotic-sounding common name because you can grow the pineapple guava in colder, temperate regions if you provide it with a sunny, sheltered, frost-free site. It will form a good-size shrub when planted next to a warm house wall in average to poor soil with very good drainage. The leaves are grey-green on the top surface and white underneath, while the 10cm (4in) wide, purple-red flowers consist of four, thick, fleshy petals. With luck, after a long hot summer, you may also be rewarded with tasty, egg-shaped fruit.

OTHER VARIETY *A. sellowiana* 'Variegata' (leaves margined with creamy-white).

PLANT PROFILE
HEIGHT 2m (6ft)
SPREAD 2.5m (8ft)
SITE Full sun
SOIL Free-draining
HARDINESS Frost hardy
FLOWERING Midsummer

A | *Acer negundo* 'Flamingo' Ash-leaved maple

FOR ITS FIRST 12 YEARS this deciduous tree is more like a shrub because it puts on only about 30cm (1ft) of height a year. If you want to keep it at that height, prune it hard each winter – this also forces plenty of colourful, new spring growth. The shoots are red and the new leaves have attractive pink margins which then turn white, but the best effects are reserved for the autumn when the leaves flare up with brilliant colours before falling. Promptly cut off shoots bearing all-green leaves or the whole plant may eventually lose its variegation.

OTHER VARIETY *A. japonicum* 'Vitifolium' (leaves turn red in autumn).

PLANT PROFILE

HEIGHT 4m (12ft) after 12 years

SPREAD 2.5m (8ft) after 12 years

SITE Full sun, partial shade

SOIL Moist, fertile, free-draining

HARDINESS Fully hardy

FLOWERING Spring

Acer palmatum 'Garnet' Japanese maple

A

THERE ARE TWO VERY GOOD REASONS for planting slow-growing Japanese maples. First, their rich autumn colours range from copper and gold to crimson and, second, they have an attractive mound-like shape. 'Garnet' forms a medium-high, sprawling set of branches with finely cut leaves that turn lavish red-purple in the autumn, and hang on slightly longer than many other maples. All Japanese maples need a slightly sheltered site, away from cold winds and spring frosts, and acid, rich, moist but free-draining soil.

OTHER VARIETIES *A. palmatum* 'Butterfly' (grey-green leaves margined white); *A. palmatum* var. *dissectum* (finely cut leaves turning gold in autumn); *A. palmatum* 'Osakazuki' (leaves turn brilliant red).

PLANT PROFILE
HEIGHT 8m (25ft)
SPREAD 10m (30ft)
SITE Sun or partial shade
SOIL Acid, fertile, moist but free-draining
HARDINESS Fully hardy
FLOWERING Mid-spring

A

Actinidia kolomikta

THIS TWINING, WOODY, DECIDUOUS CLIMBER provides lively foliage colours in the spring, plus a good autumn show. The young, heart-shaped, bronzy-purple leaves are white and then pink at the tips, and at the end of the season they turn fiery red. In between times, there are gently scented white flowers, but to get the small, edible yellow-green, gooseberry-like fruit you will need male and female plants in close proximity. Actinidia needs a position in full sun for a good display of leaf colours, and should be trained against horizontal wires on a wall. Prune for shape and to thin out the stems in late winter.

OTHER VARIETIES *A. arguta* (taller-growing, fragrant white flowers, dark green leaves); *A. deliciosa* (females produce edible fruit).

PLANT PROFILE
HEIGHT 5m (15ft)
SITE Full sun
SOIL Fertile, free-draining
HARDINESS Fully hardy
FLOWERING Early summer

Aesculus pavia 'Atrosanguinea' Red buckeye

A

TOWERING HORSE CHESTNUTS might be in this plant's genes, but red buckeye is actually a relatively modest-sized shrub or small tree. It has 13cm (5in) long, dangling, glossy leaves which turn gold in the autumn, and dark red, bottle-brush-like flowers, followed in autumn by smooth-skinned fruit. This is quite a large shrub and it is best grown in wild or woodland gardens, or you could plant it as part of a perimeter garden hedge. The red buckeye likes a sunny or partially shaded site and fertile, moist but free-draining soil.

OTHER VARIETY *A. parviflora* (smaller-growing, spidery-white flowers with protruding stamens).

PLANT PROFILE

HEIGHT 5m (15ft)

SPREAD 3m (10ft)

SITE Sun or partial shade

SOIL Moist, fertile, free-draining

HARDINESS Fully hardy

FLOWERING Early summer

A

Ailanthus altissima Tree of heaven

ALTHOUGH A LARGE TREE in its native China, in northwest Europe
it does not usually become too big. The best technique for garden
cultivation is to cut it back hard in late winter or early spring to
just above ground level, forcing up one impressive flagpole-like
stem. If other stems start growing, remove them, leaving the most
vigorous to develop. It subsequently produces a few huge leaves,
up to 90–120cm (3–4ft) long, which are divided into about 30
smaller leaflets, and makes a dramatic, architectural centrepiece for
an unusual garden design. Alternatively, you can allow a few stems
to grow, giving it a more bush-like appearance. Provide rich soil
and a sheltered position to prevent winds from ripping the foliage.

PLANT PROFILE

HEIGHT 2–2.5m (6–8ft)

SPREAD 15m (50ft)

SITE Sun or partial shade

SOIL Fertile, free-draining

HARDINESS Fully hardy

FLOWERING Summer

Akebia quinata Chocolate vine

INTERESTING AND HIGHLY DISTINCTIVE, this semi-evergreen climber produces small, vanilla-scented, brownish-purple flowers. The female flowers are about 3cm (1in) wide, and are larger than the adjacent males. Given a warm spring and a long, hot summer, it may produce fruit resembling a string of miniature sausages. It is a fast, sometimes invasive plant and needs rich, moist but well-drained soil. Though hardy, young plants also benefit from a thick mulch of compost for protection during their first winters. Grow it along horizontal wires on a wall or sturdy fence, which it will quickly cover, and prune to control growth after flowering.

OTHER VARIETY *A. trifoliata* (hanging clusters of purple flowers).

PLANT PROFILE

HEIGHT 10m (30ft)

SITE Full sun or partial shade

SOIL Fertile, moist but free-draining

HARDINESS Fully hardy

FLOWERING Early spring

A | *Aloysia triphylla* Lemon verbena

STRONGLY LEMON-SCENTED, DECIDUOUS LEAVES are this plant's most desirable feature, making it a valuable, aromatic addition to an outdoor seating area. In late summer it also produces airy sprays of tiny, pale lilac to white flowers. A Mediterranean plant, it is best planted with the protection of a warm, sunny wall to reflect light and heat, and needs poor, free-draining soil. In summer borders it helps if lemon verbena is flanked by flowers with plenty of impact and colour because it is grown for its scent, not its looks. It can also be potted up in a large container, which can be brought into a conservatory over winter. It looks particularly striking when grown as a standard, as its leaves are then conveniently at nose level. The foliage makes an excellent ingredient in pot-pourri.

PLANT PROFILE	
HEIGHT	2m (6ft)
SPREAD	2m (6ft)
SITE	Full sun
SOIL	Average, free-draining
HARDINESS	Frost hardy
FLOWERING	Late summer

Amelanchier canadensis Shadbush

A

ERECT AND MULTI-STEMMED, the shadbush is a star performer in the autumn when the leaves turn yellow, orange and then rich red, all at different times. The effect is a fantastic mix of colours. It also gives a good show in spring when it bears clusters of pure white flowers, followed by blue–black berries. Grow it in a woodland or wild garden, or at the garden's edge, in acid, moist but well–drained soil. If you have room in the garden for more than one, then try the 6m (20ft) high *Amelanchier* x *grandiflora* 'Ballerina' which has red berries that ripen to black, and equally good autumn leaf colour.

OTHER VARIETY *A. lamarckii* (taller-growing, leaves coloured orange and red).

PLANT PROFILE

HEIGHT 6m (20ft)

SPREAD 8m (25ft)

SITE Sun or partial shade

SOIL Acid, fertile, moist but free-draining

HARDINESS Fully hardy

FLOWERING Spring

A | *Amorpha fruticosa* Bastard indigo

THIN SPIKES HOLDING CLUSTERS of tiny purple-blue flowers, less than 2.5cm (1in) long, appear in late summer. In addition, this useful deciduous shrub has scented, 30cm (12in) long leaves composed of up to 33 small, oval-shaped leaflets, which make a good addition to flower arrangements. It needs light, free-draining, poor soil and is extremely hardy, thriving in difficult areas where few other shrubs will grow. Prune it in early spring, when the top growth should be removed, leaving the main structure of woody stems to carry the new season's leaves, stems and flowers.

PLANT PROFILE	
HEIGHT	5m (15ft)
SPREAD	5m (15ft)
SITE	Sun or partial shade
SOIL	Free-draining
HARDINESS	Fully hardy
FLOWERING	Late summer

Ampelopsis glandulosa var. *brevipedunculata* 'Elegans'

THIS STRIKING, ELEGANT, DECIDUOUS CLIMBER has a pleasing mix of small green leaves, splashed pink and white, with turquoise-blue berries in the autumn which are fully revealed after the foliage has fallen. 'Elegans' needs free-draining soil and a warm, sunny, sheltered site against a wall for the best fruit. It also grows well over pergolas, and looks especially effective if you allow some berrying stems to dangle down. If it is being grown up a house wall, prune the top growth annually, ensuring that it is well clear of the roof tiles and gutters which will quickly become clogged with fallen leaves.

OTHER VARIETY *A. megalophylla* (dark green leaves and green flowers followed by black fruit).

PLANT PROFILE	
HEIGHT 3m (10ft)	
SITE Sun or partial shade	
SOIL Free-draining	
HARDINESS Fully hardy	
FLOWERING Summer	

Andromeda polifolia Common bog rosemary

THIS SMALL PLANT MAKES A MOUND of leathery, evergreen leaves, similar to those of rosemary, on wiry stems. The tiny flowers appear in compact clusters at the tips of the leafy stems. Far too small to plant near large shrubs, such as rhododendrons and camellias, it is best grown with heathers, at the front of a border, or in a raised bed or rock garden. The ideal growing conditions are moist, rich, acid soil; if the soil is on the dry side, add a thick mulch of leafmould in the spring after heavy rain while the soil is still very wet.

OTHER VARIETIES *A. polifolia* 'Alba' (pure white flowers); *A. polifolia* 'Compacta' (pink flowers); *A. polifolia* 'Macrophylla' (smaller-growing, deep pink and white flowers); *A. polifolia* 'Nikko' (clear pink flowers).

PLANT PROFILE
HEIGHT 40cm (16in)
SPREAD 60cm (24in)
SITE Partial shade or full sun
SOIL Acid, moist, fertile
HARDINESS Fully hardy
FLOWERING Spring to early summer

Anisodontea capensis

FIND THE WARMEST, SUNNIEST SPOT in the garden, with shelter and good drainage, for this tender, South African evergreen. In colder areas prone to frost, it is best to grow it in a pot and bring it inside for the winter. Despite its delicate nature, it is well worth growing for its long show of 2.5cm (1in) wide, red-purple flowers, held on vertical hairy stems, which last right through the summer and into the early autumn. When the shrub is young, nip out the tips of the branches to encourage more flowering stems and a bushier, denser look. Once it is established, after a few years, a gentle annual trim in mid- or late spring is all you need do to keep it in shape.

PLANT PROFILE

HEIGHT 60cm–100cm (24in–39in)

SPREAD 40–80cm (16–32in)

SITE Full sun

SOIL Average, free-draining

HARDINESS Half hardy

FLOWERING Summer to autumn

A · *Antigonon leptopus* Confederate vine

UNUSUAL HEART-SHAPED FOLIAGE is the best feature of this quick-growing, South American evergreen vine. In ideal conditions it will flower over a long summer period and into the autumn, but in cooler, more temperate regions it tends to flower late in the summer. The flowers are typically in the coral pink-to-red range, although they can be white. Because it needs a frost-free environment over the winter, dig it up in late autumn, cut it back, and keep it potted up in an unheated greenhouse or on a cool window sill, watering only occasionally to stop the soil from drying out. The following spring, stand it outside during the day, and bring it in at night until the frosts are completely over. Then, in early summer, you can finally plant it outside again.

PLANT PROFILE

HEIGHT 5–6m (15–20ft)

SITE Full sun

SOIL Average, free-draining

HARDINESS Half hardy

FLOWERING Late summer

DECORATIVE BARK

Even before the flowers and berries appear, the attractive peeling bark of this shrub provides an additional point of interest in the garden.

Arbutus unedo f. *rubra* Strawberry tree

A

TECHNICALLY A TREE, this plant is actually branching and shrubby, and grows about 30cm (12in) a year. It has particularly attractive shedding, reddish-brown bark, and the leaves are 10cm (4in) long and glossy. The small, dark pink flowers are followed in autumn by bright red strawberry-like fruit, which explains the plant's common name. In fact, the berries start to develop the previous year, and take 12 months to fatten up and ripen. Grow the strawberry tree in rich, free-draining acid soil in a sheltered spot. 'Elfin King' is a compact form, growing 2m (6ft) high and 1.5m (5ft) wide.

OTHER VARIETY *A. andrachne* (smooth, peeling, red-brown bark, white flowers followed by orange-red berries).

PLANT PROFILE
HEIGHT 8m (25ft)
SPREAD 8m (25ft)
SITE Sun
SOIL Acid, fertile, free-draining
HARDINESS Fully hardy
FLOWERING Autumn

A

Arctostaphylos x *media* 'Wood's Red' Bearberry

ITS LOW MAXIMUM HEIGHT makes 'Wood's Red' an excellent plant for a rock garden or the front of a border where it produces a show of small, rounded, evergreen leaves. It scores high points for its large, glossy red berries which develop after the pink flowers have faded. Alternatives include 'Snow Camp' which forms a mat of stems on the ground, and has pink flowers followed by red berries, or try the white-flowered *Arctostaphylos uva-ursi* (common bearberry) which also bears scarlet berries. All need acid, moist but well-drained soil.

OTHER VARIETY *A. uva-ursi* 'Vancouver Jade' (small pink flowers).

PLANT PROFILE

HEIGHT 10cm (4in)

SPREAD 50cm (20in) or more

SITE Full sun, partial shade

SOIL Acid, moist but free-draining

HARDINESS Fully hardy

FLOWERING Late spring and early summer

Aristolochia macrophylla Dutchman's pipe

A

THIS IS ONE OF THE MOST INTRIGUING climbers. It produces small, extraordinary flowers that look like a curved, ornate, smoker's pipe with a U-bend in the middle, while the open end of each bloom has flared lips that are mottled in three colours. The only problem is that the flowers do become obscured by the large, heart-shaped, deciduous leaves and twisting, twining stems. This climber can be grown up a tree or trellis for support, and ensure that the soil is free-draining because Dutchman's pipe dislikes standing in wet winter soil. Not totally hardy, you should protect it during the winter in cold-climate gardens with a thick mulch of compost.

PLANT PROFILE

HEIGHT 8–10m (25–30ft)

SITE Sun or partial shade

SOIL Fertile, free-draining

HARDINESS Frost hardy

FLOWERING Summer

A

Aronia arbutifolia Red chokeberry

THE THREE GOOD REASONS for growing *Aronia arbutifolia* are its sprays of small, white flowers (sometimes tinged with pink) in the spring, the red berries that hang on for a long time after the flowers have finished and, finally, its wonderful autumn colour – the leaves turn orange, red, and yellow before falling. Good drainage and moist soil are the main requirements for this easy-to-grow plant. After it has flowered, prune the flowered shoots back to strong buds. On mature plants, up to one-fifth of the old shoots should be cut back to the base to encourage new, vigorous growth.

OTHER VARIETIES   *A. melanocarpa* (smaller-growing, autumn leaves turn purple-red); *A.* x *prunifolia* (autumn leaves turn dark purple-red).

PLANT PROFILE
HEIGHT 3m (10ft)
SPREAD 1.5m (5ft)
SITE Sun or partial shade
SOIL Moist but free-draining
HARDINESS Fully hardy
FLOWERING Late spring

Artemisia 'Powis Castle'

A

DUE TO ITS WOODY STEMS and shrubby habit, this perennial is often regarded as a shrub. Making a leafy clump of silver-grey foliage, it can flower but rarely does so. When flowers do appear, they are yellow-tinged and insignificant, and are usually removed. The best garden position is where the foliage sets off the brighter colours of adjacent plants. Without full sun and sharp drainage results will be poor. To promote new, vigorous growth cut 'Powis Castle' back hard in the spring when you see new shoots appearing on the old wood.

OTHER VARIETIES *A. abrotanum* (taller, grey-green aromatic leaves); *A. absinthium* (silvery-grey, silky-hairy leaves); *A. arborescens* (leaves with a fern-like appearance); *A. dracunculus* (lance-shaped, light green leaves).

PLANT PROFILE

HEIGHT 60cm (24in)

SPREAD 90cm (36in)

SITE Full sun

SOIL Free-draining

HARDINESS Frost hardy

FLOWERING Late summer

A | *Asteranthera ovata*

IN ITS NATIVE SOUTH AMERICA, *Asteranthera ovata* may shoot up to about 4m (12ft) high, but in more temperate regions this evergreen climbing shrub will be lucky to gain a height of 45cm (18in). It will spread and creep twice this length, however, provided it is grown in moist, acid soil and given a sheltered spot in the garden with some shade. A position at the base of a wall is ideal. In return, it produces flared, reddish-pink tubular flowers, offset by small dark green leaves on white, hairy stems. This is a quirky, highly unusual plant, but it must be given the right conditions if it is to thrive.

PLANT PROFILE

HEIGHT 45cm (18in)

SPREAD 90cm (36in)

SITE Partial shade

SOIL Acid, moist

HARDINESS Frost hardy

FLOWERING Summer

Aucuba japonica 'Variegata' Spotted laurel

A

THESE TOTALLY RELIABLE EVERGREEN SHRUBS have a smart, solid appearance and a leafy covering from top to toe. All laurels flower, but for berries you need male and female plants. 'Variegata' is a female and gives bright red berries. Other good variegated forms include 'Gold Dust' and 'Crotonifolia', both with yellow-speckled leaves, while 'Crassifolia' is male and plain green. The all-greens are very versatile and grow happily just about anywhere, from full sun to dark shade, while the variegated types prefer dappled shade.

OTHER VARIETIES   *A. japonica* f. *longifolia* 'Salicifolia' (female with slender leaves); *A. japonica* 'Picturata' (female with yellow-centred leaves); *A. japonica* 'Rozannie' (compact, dark green leaves, bisexual flowers).

PLANT PROFILE	
HEIGHT 3m (10ft)	
SPREAD 3m (10ft)	
SITE Partial shade	
SOIL Average	
HARDINESS Fully hardy	
FLOWERING Mid-spring	

A | *Azara serrata*

UPRIGHT AND EVERGREEN, this shrub has glossy leaves and is grown for its profuse, sweetly scented, dark yellow flowers that look like small balls of radiating bristles. In long, hot summers, the flowers are followed by tiny mauve or white berries. It is slightly tender, and is best grown against a sunny wall where it will benefit from the extra warmth and protection, in rich, moist but free-draining soil. Prune for shape and size in late winter or early spring. *Azara microphylla* is the hardiest azara, and produces scented, greenish-yellow flowers in late winter and spring – it is also happy when grown in shade.

OTHER VARIETIES *A. dentata* (fragrant, dark yellow flowers); *A. lanceolata* (lance-shaped, bright green leaves); *A. petiolaris* (leathery, dark green leaves, creamy-yellow flowers in mid-spring).

PLANT PROFILE
HEIGHT 4m (12ft)
SPREAD 3m (10ft)
SITE Sun or partial shade
SOIL Moist, fertile, free-draining
HARDINESS Frost hardy
FLOWERING Midsummer

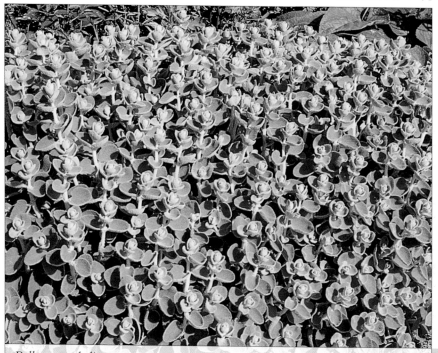

Ballota pseudodictamnus

B

THIS IS A KEY PLANT for gravel or Mediterranean-style gardens, and flourishes in a hot, sunny position with its roots in quite poor, free-draining soil. The stems bear small, felted, greyish-yellow-green leaves, each about 3cm (1¼in) long, and end in attractive rosettes at the tips. The hotter the summer, the more felted the leaves become. Grow it in free-draining soil with some shelter because it is not fully hardy. In midsummer, cut back the entire plant, and it will quickly produce a fresh batch of leaves that last well through the winter.

OTHER VARIETIES *B. acetabulosa* (taller-growing, small, purple-pink flowers with white marks); *B.* 'All Hallows Green' (woolly lime-green leaves, small, pale green flowers in mid- and late summer).

PLANT PROFILE	
HEIGHT 45cm (18in)	
SPREAD 60cm (24in)	
SITE Full sun	
SOIL Free-draining	
HARDINESS Frost hardy	
FLOWERING Late spring and early summer	

B *Berberidopsis corallina* Coral plant

THIS WOODY, EVERGREEN, SCRAMBLING CLIMBER from Chile is ideal for a sheltered wall, out of direct sunlight, where it will not be flayed by cold winds. The dark green leaves grow up to 10cm (4in) long, and nicely set off the tiny pearl-like, dark red flowers that dangle like cherries. It is slightly fussy in its requirements and needs humus-rich soil, while the roots demand a thick mulch of compost for protection in winter. This is not a vigorous climber and it needs to be trained against horizontal wires attached to a supporting surface, although you can also encourage it to scramble up an old, stout tree. Prune in the spring to thin out congested growth.

PLANT PROFILE

HEIGHT 5m (15ft)

SITE Partial shade

SOIL Moist, free-draining

HARDINESS Frost hardy

FLOWERING Summer to early autumn

Berberis darwinii

B

A HIGH–QUALITY EVERGREEN, this berberis puts on a show of bright orange flowers early in the year, followed by a mass of blue-black berries in the autumn. It makes a prickly, medium-high hedge or divider within the garden, growing about 30cm (12in) in height a year. Plant the shrubs for a hedge about 45cm (18in) apart. Like most berberis, *Berberis darwinii* grows just about anywhere in the garden, except on clay. Prune for shape only immediately after flowering.

OTHER VARIETIES *B.* 'Goldilocks' (red-stalked, golden-yellow flowers); *B.* x *lologensis* 'Apricot Queen' (dark orange flowers); *B.* 'Red Jewel' (dark bronze-red young leaves, yellow flowers).

PLANT PROFILE
HEIGHT 3m (10ft)
SPREAD 3m (10ft)
SITE Full sun or partial shade
SOIL Free-draining
HARDINESS Fully hardy
FLOWERING Mid- and late spring

B *Berberis thunbergii* 'Bagatelle'

FOR THE FRONT OF A BORDER this berberis is hard to beat. The pale
yellow flowers are followed by shiny red berries, and in the autumn
the leaves flare orange and red. 'Bagatelle' is small and compact, and
produces a good effect when grown beside a path, or alternated
with a box ball or an oval, evergreen, dwarf conifer. It needs only an
occasional trim in late winter to keep it in shape, but beware of the
spiny stems when pruning. For the best leaf colour, flowering and
berrying, grow it in full sun and free-draining soil.

OTHER VARIETIES *B. thunbergii* f. *atropurpurea* (red-purple foliage,
turning red in autumn); *B. thunbergii* 'Atropurpurea Nana' (red-purple
foliage); *B. thunbergii* 'Rose Glow' (white-flecked, red-purple foliage).

PLANT PROFILE
HEIGHT 30cm (12in)
SPREAD 40cm (16in)
SITE Full sun
SOIL Free-draining
HARDINESS Fully hardy
FLOWERING Spring

Bignonia capreolata Cross vine

ALTHOUGH MAGNIFICENT AND RAMPANT, this rapid climber is on the tender side. In ideal conditions – a sunny, sheltered, frost-free site with free-draining soil, where its roots are not locked in cold, wet soil all winter – cross vine will produce large, evergreen leaves. Protected city centre gardens often provide a suitable environment. The bright, orange-red, trumpet-shaped flowers are small yet highly attractive. The tendrils need some form of support to latch on to, and this can be provided by horizontal wires attached to a wall, or by a host tree with twiggy growth at the bottom. Cross vine can also be grown in a conservatory, but you need to make sure there is a long stretch of wall for it to colonize.

B

PLANT PROFILE

HEIGHT 10m (30ft)

SITE Full sun

SOIL Free-draining

HARDINESS Half hardy

FLOWERING Summer

B | *Billardiera longiflora* Purple apple berry

SUITABLE ONLY FOR MILD GARDENS, this small, unusual, eye-catching Australian climber never becomes too rampant. Its best feature is its liberal covering of electric purple-blue berries in early autumn, although sometimes berries can also be coloured purple, red, pink, or white. It needs to be grown in a sunny, sheltered part of the garden, ideally against a wall, and in free-draining soil to prevent the stem rotting in winter. If you have sufficient space for it in a warm conservatory, the display of flowers and berries will be even better. In the garden, allow its wiry stems to sprint over adjoining plants.

OTHER VARIETY *B. scandens* (bell-shaped greenish-yellow or violet to purple flowers, followed by olive-green berries).

PLANT PROFILE
HEIGHT 2–3m (6–10ft)
SITE Sun or partial shade
SOIL Free-draining
HARDINESS Frost hardy
FLOWERING Summer

Bomarea caldasii

THIS TENDER, DECIDUOUS CLIMBER comes from South America and needs to be grown either in a conservatory or in a warm, sheltered, frost-free spot outdoors. When happy, it produces clusters of flowers, each like a small tube. The blooms are dark reddish–terracotta on the outside and orange-yellow with scores of tiny spots inside. It needs moist but well-drained soil, and some protection over winter to keep off the rain. In late winter, cut back to ground level all dead top-growth and stems that have flowered. *B. hirtella* also requires a frost-free site, and flowers well.

OTHER VARIETIES *B. hirtella* (orange-green flowers); *B. salsilla* (hardier, reddish-green flowers).

PLANT PROFILE

HEIGHT 3–4m (10–12ft)

SITE Full sun

SOIL Moist but free-draining

HARDINESS Half hardy

FLOWERING Late spring to autumn

B *Brachyglottis* (Dunedin Group) 'Sunshine'

MAKING A PLUMP, EVERGREEN, SPRAWLING mound of silver-grey leaves when young, with white hairs underneath, 'Sunshine' thrives in free-draining soil, especially in coastal sites. In summer it is richly coloured with a bold show of yellow flowers, and can be pruned after flowering to give it a good shape and to prevent it running into neighbouring plants. Where wind protection is required, you can plant several shrubs to make a highly effective hedge. It can also be used as a contrast for adjacent climbers, such as a clematis with red flowers, which will stand out against the yellow.

OTHER VARIETIES *B. compacta* (compact, mound-forming); *B. monroi* (densely growing, leathery, olive-green leaves).

PLANT PROFILE

HEIGHT 1–1.5m (3–5ft)

SPREAD 2m (6ft) or more

SITE Partial shade

SOIL Free-draining

HARDINESS Fully hardy

FLOWERING Early to midsummer

Cut off a non-flowering shoot, with 2-3 leaf pairs, just below a set of leaves. Trim off the tip, just above a pair of leaves, and then remove the lower leaves. Then cut the remaining leaves in half.

Buddleja alternifolia

B

THIS IS A BUDDLEJA WITH A DIFFERENCE because it can be trained as a single-stem shrub, with a mass of weeping branches bearing lilac flowers growing from the top. Stand it apart from other plants so that it can be better appreciated. You can also grow it in the traditional way as a dense, deciduous shrub, or site it against a wall. The arching stems give it an elegant look, and the richly scented flowers attract bees and butterflies. Deadhead and prune after flowering, removing one-quarter of the stems. It does best on free-draining or chalky soil.

OTHER VARIETIES *B. davidii* 'Fascinating' (lilac-pink flowers); *B.* 'Lochinch' (later-flowering, orange-eyed, violet-blue flowers).

PLANT PROFILE	
HEIGHT 4m (12ft)	
SPREAD 4m (12ft)	
SITE Full sun	
SOIL Free-draining	
HARDINESS Fully hardy	
FLOWERING Early summer	

B

Buddleja davidii 'Black Knight' Butterfly bush

FLOWERING IN MID- AND LATE SUMMER, 'Black Knight' puts on an astonishing show of dark purple-blue flowers with a heavy, fragrant scent. Never neat and tidy, stems shoot out in different directions, especially after a spring prune. If you deadhead it promptly there may be a second flush of smaller flowers. This deciduous shrub likes free-draining soil and is virtually indestructible, self-seeding on any patch of poor soil. If space permits, it makes a fine contrast beside the equally vigorous *Buddleja davidii* 'White Profusion'.

OTHER VARIETIES *B. davidii* 'Dartmoor' (reddish-purple flowers); *B. davidii* 'Harlequin' (red-purple flowers, cream-margined leaves); *B. davidii* 'White Bouquet' (white flowers with a yellow eye).

PLANT PROFILE	
HEIGHT 3m (10ft)	
SPREAD 5m (15ft)	
SITE Full sun	
SOIL Poor, free-draining	
HARDINESS Fully hardy	
FLOWERING Summer to autumn	

Buddleja globosa Orange ball tree

B

A DISTINCTIVE DECIDUOUS OR SEMI-EVERGREEN shrub, this buddleja has early summer flowers that resemble small, orange golf balls, and is best grown in a sheltered site where you can really appreciate their scent. After flowering, remove the spent blooms and the top 8cm (3in) of stems, plus any wayward growth, but keep pruning to a minimum or you will lose the following year's flowers. You can use the orange ball tree as a support for annual climbers which will disguise the bare stems that can form at the base. Alternatively, place it toward the back of a border where these stems cannot be seen.

PLANT PROFILE	
HEIGHT 5m (15ft)	
SPREAD 5m (15ft)	
SITE Full sun	
SOIL Free-draining	
HARDINESS Frost hardy	
FLOWERING Early summer	

B | *Bupleurum fruticosum* Shrubby hare's ear

THIS SOUND, RELIABLE CHOICE for coastal gardens makes a medium-sized, dense, rounded, evergreen shrub with 8cm (3in) long, blue-tinged leaves and sprays of tiny yellow flowers. Its main use is as a background linking shrub rather than as a star performer. Shrubby hare's ear is not totally hardy, and requires a sunny, sheltered position where it will not be subjected to hard frosts, but it is not very fussy about the soil, provided it is free-draining. Lightly prune for shape in mid-spring, but if it does become overgrown and shapeless, cut it back hard at the same time of year.

OTHER VARIETY *B. angulosum* (smaller-growing, yellow or creamy-green flowers surrounded by jade-green bracts).

PLANT PROFILE
HEIGHT 2m (6ft)
SPREAD 2.5m (8ft)
SITE Full sun
SOIL Free-draining
HARDINESS Frost hardy
FLOWERING Midsummer to early autumn

BOX SUCKER

In mid-spring, infestations of flattened, pale green, aphid-like, sap-sucking insects appear and cause leaves to curl, creating stunted, cabbage-like growth. Spray or remove the affected stems.

Buxus sempervirens 'Latifolia Maculata' Common box

B

ONE OF THE BEST SHRUBS for edging and topiary, common box can be pruned to create a wide range of shapes – from geometric pyramids and squares to animal forms – as well as low hedges for a knot garden or parterre. 'Latifolia Maculata' is an attractive variety, with bright yellow early summer foliage that turns a darker green with yellow markings as the season advances. Old plants can be rejuvenated very easily by pruning hard in spring (when they also need a feed), while hedging and edging should be trimmed in the summer. Water young plants well during dry spells.

OTHER VARIETIES *B. sempervirens* 'Elegantissima' (white-margined leaves); *B. sempervirens* 'Suffruticosa' (compact, good for low hedges).

PLANT PROFILE	
HEIGHT 2.5m (8ft)	
SPREAD 2m (6ft)	
SITE Partial shade	
SOIL Fertile, free-draining	
HARDINESS Fully hardy	
FLOWERING Late spring	

C | *Caesalpina pulcherrima* Barbados pride

GIVEN A SUNNY, SHELTERED SITE, Barbados pride is quite a beauty, but it can be tricky to grow because it is only just half hardy and will die if caught by frost. It produces bright green, feathery foliage that hangs on throughout the winter, provided it is kept in a warm environment. If you do grow this shrub outside, dig it up and bring it indoors in a large pot as soon as temperatures approach freezing in the autumn; alternatively, treat it as a conservatory plant. Moving it indoors for winter means that it will never grow large, but you will be compensated by the hint of exotica it brings to the garden in the summer. Give it a gentle trim after flowering, if required.

OTHER VARIETY *C. gilliesii* (smaller-growing, yellow flowers).

PLANT PROFILE

HEIGHT 3–6m (10–20ft)

SPREAD 2–4m (6–12ft)

SITE Full sun

SOIL Moist, fertile, free-draining

HARDINESS Half hardy

FLOWERING Spring to autumn

Callicarpa bodinieri var. *giraldii* 'Profusion'

C

THERE IS A PURPLE-MAUVE FLASH OF COLOUR just before the leaves fall in autumn when the branches are studded with violet, pearl-like berries that persist into winter. They make this a star performer for the late-season garden. 'Profusion' also gets off to a lively start in spring with new bronze-coloured leaves that turn green over the summer. An erect shrub, 'Profusion' has stiff woody stems, and likes free-draining soil. To keep it vigorous and free-berrying, prune one in five stems to the ground each spring to encourage new growth.

OTHER VARIETIES *C. bodinieri* var. *giraldii* (pink flowers, dark green leaves); *C. dichotoma* (smaller-growing, pale pink flowers followed by dark lilac fruit); *C. japonica* 'Leucocarpa' (white flowers and fruit).

PLANT PROFILE
HEIGHT 3m (10ft)
SPREAD 2.5m (8ft)
SITE Full sun or dappled shade
SOIL Free-draining
HARDINESS Fully hardy
FLOWERING Midsummer

C

Callistemon citrinus 'Splendens' **Crimson bottlebrush**

AUSTRALIAN BOTTLEBRUSHES ARE FUN PLANTS, making large shrubs with cylindrical, tactile flowers consisting of scores of bristle-like stamens. Their hardiness varies, and this evergreen belongs to the tender category. It can be grown and kept small in a pot which should be brought into a conservatory or heated greenhouse over winter. It needs free-draining, moderately fertile, neutral to acid soil, and can be pruned lightly after flowering to give an attractive shape, although you can be more ruthless in spring if it grows too large. For a permanent border plant, try the hardier *C. subulatus*.

OTHER VARIETIES *C. pallidus* (smaller-growing, greenish-yellow flowers); *C. salignus* (white flowers); *C. sieberi* (creamy-yellow flowers).

PLANT PROFILE
HEIGHT 2–8m (6–25ft)
SPREAD 1.5–6m (5–20ft)
SITE Full sun
SOIL Free-draining
HARDINESS Half hardy
FLOWERING Spring and summer

Calluna vulgaris 'Firefly' Scotch heather

C

THE PERFECT PLACE for growing evergreen heathers is in a border with acid soil. 'Firefly' has terracotta-coloured leaves in the summer which turn dark brick-red over winter. It mixes well with golden-yellow 'Sir John Charrington' which has orange and red winter foliage, and copper-red 'Glenfiddich' which turns bronze-red when temperatures fall. If the height of heathers is too uniform, combine them with conifers for variety. All callunas are easy to grow in rich, free-draining soil, and will need just a gentle trim in early spring, although excessively long leaves can be snipped off at any time.

OTHER VARIETIES *C. vulgaris* 'Beoley Silver' (silver foliage, white flowers); *C. vulgaris* 'Darkness' (crimson flowers).

PLANT PROFILE

HEIGHT 45cm (18in)

SPREAD 75cm (30in)

SITE Full sun

SOIL Acid, fertile, free-draining

HARDINESS Fully hardy

FLOWERING Midsummer to late autumn

C

Calycanthus floridus Carolina allspice

FOR ANY SCENTED GARDEN, the deciduous Carolina allspice is an important component. It emits a rich, fruity scent from its leaves (when rubbed), bark and small, dark red flowers. The blooms also resemble waterlilies, while the attractive dark green leaves are covered with downy wool beneath, and turn yellow before falling in the autumn. Make sure that the soil is moist and rich, and for the best results provide a warm, sheltered site. Prune in early spring by cutting back hard to the base framework of oldest wood in order to prompt new, vigorous growth.

OTHER VARIETY *C. occidentalis* (red flowers with brown-tipped petals).

PLANT PROFILE	
HEIGHT	2.5m (8ft)
SPREAD	3m (10ft)
SITE	Sun
SOIL	Moist, fertile
HARDINESS	Fully hardy
FLOWERING	Summer

Camellia x *williamsii* 'Donation'

C

ONE OF THE MOST VERSATILE CAMELLIAS, this is a tough, erect shrub with an eye-catching show of semi-double pink flowers which are even darker and longer lasting when grown in partial shade. Like all camellias, it needs a sheltered position away from cold winds and from the early morning sun so that frosted flower buds thaw slowly and are not damaged. Camellias also require acid soil which should be mulched with compost to stop it from drying out.

OTHER VARIETIES *C. japonica* 'Bob's Tinsie' (small, brilliant red flowers); *C. japonica* 'Elegans' (large, rose-pink flowers); *C. sasanqua* 'Narumigata' (pink-tinged white flowers); *C.* x *williamsii* 'Anticipation' (very large crimson flowers); *C.* x *williamsii* 'St Ewe' (rose-pink flowers).

PLANT PROFILE

HEIGHT 5m (15ft)

SPREAD 2.5m (8ft)

SITE Light shade

SOIL Moist, fertile, free-draining

HARDINESS Fully hardy

FLOWERING Late winter to late spring

C

Campsis x *tagliabuana* 'Madame Galen' Trumpet vine

IF YOU HAVE A SUNNY, SHELTERED WALL then this deciduous climber
will erupt with richly coloured, trumpet-shaped flowers, about
23cm (9in) long. The warmer and more sheltered its position the
better, because 'Madame Galen' needs a long, hot summer to excel.
Naturally vigorous, it requires poor to average soil which must not
dry out over summer. Cutting back young climbers just after
planting, leaving just 20cm (8in) of growth, forces them to produce
new, bushy stems, while established plants can be pruned hard in late
winter, cutting back sideshoots to leave just three buds at the base.

OTHER VARIETIES *C. grandiflora* (dark orange to red flowers);
C. radicans f. *flava* (yellow flowers).

PLANT PROFILE
HEIGHT 10m (30ft)
SITE Full sun
SOIL Average, moist
HARDINESS Frost hardy
FLOWERING Late summer to autumn

Cantua buxifolia Sacred flower of the Incas

C

THIS EXOTIC SOUTH AMERICAN PLANT is a tender shrub with quite specific growing requirements. It needs a hot, sunny position, rich, moist but well-drained soil, and protection from cold winds, but find the right spot and you will be rewarded in spring with a liberal covering of dangling, tubular, fuchsia-like, pink to purple flowers. If you don't have the right conditions in the garden, it can be grown in a conservatory and trained against a wall for support. The best time to prune it is after flowering, when it needs just a light trim to maintain its shape and restrict it to the available space.

PLANT PROFILE
HEIGHT 2–5m (6–15ft)
SPREAD 1.5–2.5m (5–8ft)
SITE Full sun
SOIL Fertile, moist but free-draining
HARDINESS Half hardy
FLOWERING Spring

C | *Carpenteria californica*

THIS SUPERB EVERGREEN has papery, peeling, beige-coloured bark and glossy, leathery leaves up to 12cm (5in) long. In early summer there is an arresting show of circular, gently scented white flowers with yellow centres. It is hardy in mild areas, but still needs to bask in the hottest, most sheltered part of the garden in free-draining soil. 'Ladhams' Variety' has slightly larger white flowers, up to 8cm (3in) wide, while the more compact 'Elizabeth' has smaller ones. Prune after flowering, if necessary, to maintain its shape.

OTHER VARIETY *C. californica* 'Bodnant' (similar flowers and leaves to *C. californica* but hardier).

PLANT PROFILE	
HEIGHT 2m (6ft) or more	
SPREAD 2m (6ft)	
SITE Full sun	
SOIL Free-draining	
HARDINESS Frost hardy	
FLOWERING Early and midsummer	

Caryopteris x *clandonensis* 'Heavenly Blue'

C

THE RICH BLUE FLOWERS on erect stems bring the front or middle of a border to life in the second half of summer. The grey-green leaves, silvery beneath, of this bushy deciduous shrub release a pungent scent if rubbed, and make a wonderful foil for the flowers. Where growing a couple, include 'Dark Knight' with its silvery leaves and dark blue flowers. Caryopteris look good against gravel, and thrive in sunny gardens with well-drained soil. In mid- to late spring cut back the stems to within a few buds of the main framework.

OTHER VARIETIES *C.* x *clandonensis* 'Kew Blue' (dark blue flowers, grey-green leaves); *C.* x *clandonensis* 'Worcester Gold' (yellow leaves, pale blue flowers); *C. incana* (bright violet-blue, sometimes white, flowers).

PLANT PROFILE
HEIGHT 1m (3ft)
SPREAD 1m (3ft)
SITE Full sun
SOIL Free-draining
HARDINESS Fully hardy
FLOWERING Late summer and early autumn

C | *Cassiope* 'Edinburgh'

SMALL AND EVERGREEN, this front-of-border shrub has wiry stems with scale-like, dark green leaves and small, delicate-looking, bell-shaped, white flowers. It is suitable for a rock garden, or plant it beneath trees in a woodland-style setting, but in both cases ensure that the soil is acid and moist, while the site must be sheltered if cassiope is to thrive. *Cassiope lycopodioides* also has white flowers, but is even shorter, reaching just 8cm (3in) high, with a spreading habit.

OTHER VARIETIES *C. lycopodioides* 'Beatrice Lilley' (dwarf, compact variety); *C.* 'Muirhead' (white flowers, silvery leaves).

PLANT PROFILE	
HEIGHT To 25cm (10in)	
SPREAD To 25cm (10in)	
SITE Partial shade or sun	
SOIL Acid, moist	
HARDINESS Fully hardy	
FLOWERING Late spring	

Ceanothus 'Blue Mound' California lilac

GIVEN THE RIGHT CONDITIONS, some California lilacs make massive plants, typically with a covering of blue flowers, although they also come in pink and white. This medium-high evergreen shrub forms a mound and has dark green leaves. It needs sun, shelter and free-draining soil, for example, against a wall in a gravel garden. Prune after flowering, either lightly or, if overgrown, by cutting back the flowered shoots by one-third to a half. Young plants benefit from a thick winter mulch of compost in their first few years.

OTHER VARIETIES *C.* 'Autumnal Blue' (taller, sky-blue flowers); *C.* 'Burkwoodii' (later-flowering, bright blue flowers); *C.* 'Cascade' (powder-blue flowers); *C.* 'Southmead' (dark, rich blue flowers).

PLANT PROFILE	
HEIGHT 1.5m (5ft)	
SPREAD 2m (6ft)	
SITE Full sun	
SOIL Free-draining	
HARDINESS Frost hardy	
FLOWERING Late spring	

C | *Celastrus orbiculatus* Oriental bittersweet

THIS DECIDUOUS, RAMPANT, TWINING CLIMBER needs a large, strong structure to romp up – a wall, well-built pergola or stout tree are all good options. The summer flowers are quite small and not especially noteworthy, but the seed capsules are a real bonus. They are yellow, like the leaves when they change colour in the autumn, and split open to reveal tiny seeds that are usually pink or orange-red. The capsules have a huge visual impact in the autumn, and although separate male and female plants are required to get to this stage, some nurseries offer Hermaphrodite Group which produces seed without a partner. Grow these plants in free-draining soil, in either full sun or partial shade.

PLANT PROFILE

HEIGHT 14m (46ft)

SITE Full sun, partial shade

SOIL Free-draining

HARDINESS Fully hardy

FLOWERING Summer

Ceratostigma willmottianum Chinese plumbago

C

OF ALL THE TYPES OF PLUMBAGO, this is the hardiest and best choice. A deciduous, vigorous shrub, in late summer it is liberally covered in mid-blue flowers which are offset by red-tinted autumn foliage. Although hardy, cold winters can cause the stems to die back, but if you prune it down to the ground in spring it quickly rejuvenates, sending up dozens of new stems. To help it survive cold winters, make sure that the soil is free-draining because the roots hate being locked in wet soil, and give it a sunny, protected position.

OTHER VARIETIES *C. griffithii* (frost hardy, red-stemmed, mid-green leaves with purple margins); *C. plumbaginoides* (smaller-growing, spikes of brilliant blue flowers).

PLANT PROFILE
HEIGHT 1m (3ft)
SPREAD 1.5m (5ft)
SITE Full sun
SOIL Free-draining
HARDINESS Fully hardy
FLOWERING Late summer and autumn

C | *Cercis canadensis* 'Forest Pansy' Eastern redbud

STRICTLY SPEAKING THIS IS A SPREADING TREE, but in its early years 'Forest Pansy' has very shrubby growth. The leaves are its most impressive feature. Heart-shaped and rich reddish-purple, they add a dash of colour in summer, and because they look particularly bright when backlit, ensure that the sun is behind them for part of the day. If the plant grows too large, prune it back annually to near ground level, leaving just 2–3 buds at the base, or cut off the crown where most of the stems meet the trunk (known as pollarding) in early spring. These pruning methods also produce the best show of leaves.

OTHER VARIETIES *C. canadensis* (bronze leaves turning yellow in autumn); *C. chinensis* (smaller-growing, green leaves turning yellow).

PLANT PROFILE
HEIGHT 10m (30ft)
SPREAD 10m (30ft)
SITE Full sun or dappled shade
SOIL Moist, fertile, free-draining
HARDINESS Fully hardy
FLOWERING Spring

Cestrum parqui Willow-leaved jasmine

C

THE BEST REASON for growing the sweetly scented willow-leaved jasmine is that you can place it close to outdoor dining areas. It does not look particularly exotic – in fact, the flowers are a pallid yellow-green – but this plant is definitely on the tender side. Provide it with a sunny, sheltered spot in the garden, and rich, free-draining soil. If the top-growth does die back during a hard winter, new shoots should emerge from the base in the following spring.

OTHER VARIETIES *C. fasciculatum* (bright red flowers, dark green, wavy edged leaves); *C.* 'Newellii' (taller-growing, crimson flowers often followed by purple-red berries).

PLANT PROFILE

HEIGHT 2m (6ft)

SPREAD 2m (6ft)

SITE Sun or partial shade

SOIL Fertile, free-draining

HARDINESS Frost hardy

FLOWERING Summer to autumn

C

Chaenomeles x *superba* 'Pink Lady' Flowering quince

ONE OF THE BEST SIGHTS in the spring garden is a wall-trained quince with stiff, bare, woody stems and dark pink flowers. Alternatively, you can grow it as a tangled, freestanding bush. It will be happy in average soil, and does well in shade or sun, although it will flower and fruit better in a light position. 'Fire Dance' is good companion plant because it adds bright red flowers to the pink. If you are growing it against a wall, use the stems as a sturdy support for a flowering clematis which will happily clamber up through it.

OTHER VARIETIES *C. speciosa* 'Moerloosei' (white flowers, flushed pink); *C.* x *superba* 'Crimson and Gold' (compact, dark red flowers with yellow centres); *C.* x *superba* 'Knap Hill Scarlet' (large red flowers).

PLANT PROFILE	
HEIGHT 1.5m (5ft)	
SPREAD 2m (6ft)	
SITE Sun or light shade	
SOIL Average, free-draining	
HARDINESS Fully hardy	
FLOWERING Spring	

Chimonanthus praecox Wintersweet

C

THIS MUST-HAVE PLANT for the second half of winter has spicy-scented, bell-shaped, lemon-yellow flowers, 2.5cm (1in) wide, that appear on the bare stems. Don't despair if a new plant does not flower in its first winter because it may take up to five years to bloom. While it makes a vigorous, freestanding shrub, it will grow taller against a sunny wall where it also benefits from the extra shelter and warmth. Plant it in moderately fertile, free-draining soil and prune the flowered stems of wall-trained plants immediately after blooming, leaving just three leaves on each.

OTHER VARIETIES *C. praecox* 'Grandiflorus' (deep yellow flowers with maroon stripes inside); *C. praecox* var. 'Luteus' (yellow, wide flowers).

PLANT PROFILE	
HEIGHT 4m (12ft)	
SPREAD 3m (10ft)	
SITE Full sun	
SOIL Free-draining	
HARDINESS Fully hardy	
FLOWERING Winter	

C | *Chionanthus virginicus* Fringe tree

THIS ATTRACTIVE, DECIDUOUS SHRUB or small tree has large, dark green glossy leaves that turn yellow in the autumn before falling. The fringe tree deserves to be far more popular than it is, not least for its gently scented, wispy white flowers which are followed, with luck, by small, blue-black fruit. The longer and hotter the summer, the better the display is likely to be. It is easy to grow, and likes free-draining soil and a sunny position. Prune the fringe tree in the late winter or early spring, when necessary, to maintain its shape or size.

OTHER VARIETY *C. retusus* (peeling or deeply furrowed bark, fragrant white flowers).

PLANT PROFILE	
HEIGHT 3m (10ft)	
SPREAD 3m (10ft) or more	
SITE Full sun	
SOIL Fertile, free-draining	
HARDINESS Fully hardy	
FLOWERING Summer	

Prune your choisya after flowering in early summer. Cutting back the stems by about 25–30cm (10–12in) will encourage a second flush of flowers later in the summer or autumn.

Choisya ternata Mexican orange blossom

C

THIS FABULOUS EVERGREEN has finger-like foliage and is studded with open, scented, starry white blooms. The main burst of flowers appears in late spring but, especially in warm, sheltered sites, it will bloom again later in the year. Mexican orange blossom is a rounded shrub, requiring only an occasional prune to keep it tidy. It looks particularly good when planted with *Crocosmia* 'Lucifer' spearing its tomato red flowers up through the front of the shrub, and if you grow it against a sunny, sheltered wall, the rich, sweet scent of the flowers will linger in the air.

OTHER VARIETIES C. 'Aztec Pearl' (pink-tinged white flowers); *C. ternata* 'Sundance' (bright yellow young leaves, white flowers).

PLANT PROFILE

HEIGHT To 2.5m (8ft)

SPREAD To 2.5m (8ft)

SITE Full sun

SOIL Fertile, free-draining

HARDINESS Fully hardy

FLOWERING Late spring, and again, with fewer flowers, in summer and autumn

C | *Chusquea culeou*

YOU WILL NEED A BIG GARDEN to accommodate this great, thicket–forming bamboo. It makes an incredibly impressive clump when growing out of its own bed in the middle of a lawn, looking like it has erupted out of the ground. It prefers rich soil and needs to be well watered during its first season to help it develop a good root system, but never plant it close to a pond, especially one with an artificial sheet lining, in case the new canes spear up through the base and cause a leak. If new canes emerge too far from the clump, slice them off at ground level with a spade. Old canes can be sawn off in the spring, just below the surface to prevent the stumps from protruding, while an occasional pruning allows air and light into the centre of the clump. Feed with a general fertilizer in the spring.

PLANT PROFILE

HEIGHT 6m (20ft)

SPREAD 2.5m (8ft)

SITE Sun or partial shade

SOIL Fertile

HARDINESS Fully hardy

Cistus x *argenteus* 'Peggy Sammons' Rock rose

C

SUN-LOVING AND STRONG-GROWING, this evergreen rock rose gives an excellent show of dark pink flowers all summer. Each flower lasts only one day, if that, but is replaced by others in rapid succession. 'Peggy Sammons' thrives in hot sun in poor, sandy soil with good drainage, and needs shelter from cold winter winds. In cold areas, provide a thick, protective winter mulch of compost. It is a short-lived plant and needs replacing every few years, or you can take cuttings in the early summer.

OTHER VARIETIES *C.* x *corbariensis* (white flowers from red buds); *C. ladanifer* (taller-growing, white flowers); *C.* x *pulverulentus* 'Sunset' (rose-pink flowers with yellow centres); *C.* x *skanbergii* (pink flowers).

PLANT PROFILE	
HEIGHT	1m (3ft)
SPREAD	1m (3ft)
SITE	Full sun
SOIL	Poor, free-draining
HARDINESS	Frost hardy
FLOWERING	Summer

C

Clematis alpina 'Frances Rivis'

FEATURING NODDING, MID-BLUE FLOWERS, 8cm (3in) wide, followed by fluffy seedheads, this exquisite climber gives any spring garden a graceful lift. It tolerates exposed sites, and makes a beautiful contrast when trained through a pink or red flowering quince (*Chaenomeles*) which flowers at the same time. The roots like shaded, moist, rich soil, while the flowers prefer to have their heads in the sun. Plant all clematis with the root ball 8cm (3in) below soil level to safeguard against disease and to promote strong, new shoots low down.

OTHER VARIETY *C. macropetala* (blue or violet-blue flowers).

PLANT PROFILE

HEIGHT 3m (10ft)

SPREAD 1.5m (5ft)

SITE Full sun

SOIL Moist, fertile

HARDINESS Fully hardy

FLOWERING Mid- to late spring

Clematis armandii 'Apple Blossom'

C

THERE ARE TWO GOOD REASONS for growing this plant: it produces pink-tinged flowers with a scent of vanilla, and has evergreen, long, dark green leaves. Plant it in a sheltered, sunny position to prevent the young bronze leaves from being ruined, or even killed, by cold winds, and to protect the flower buds from frost damage. A sheltered site also ensures that the flower scent lingers in the air. The roots need to be in shaded, moist, rich soil, and the flowers in the sun. Prune to keep it in check immediately after flowering.

OTHER VARIETY *C. alpina* (blue flowers followed by fluffy seedheads).

PLANT PROFILE	
HEIGHT 5m (15ft)	
SPREAD 3m (10ft)	
SITE Full sun	
SOIL Moist, fertile	
HARDINESS Frost hardy	
FLOWERING Early spring	

C

Clematis 'Bill MacKenzie'

NOTED FOR ITS MASS OF SMALL FLOWERS followed by a superb show of silvery seedheads, this clematis needs to be planted where its flowers receive full sun while its roots enjoy moist shade. Grow it on the cool side of an old stout tree, for example, and train the stems around to the sunny side and up into the branches. You can also let it run over a large old tree stump. Pruning is not required for aerial flowers, but for blooms closer to the base of the stems, cut them back to 20cm (8in) above the ground in early spring.

OTHER VARIETIES *C. flammula* (star-shaped, scented, white flowers); *C. tangutica* (bell-shaped, yellow flowers); *C. viticella* (bell-shaped, blue, purple, or rose-red flowers with yellow centres).

PLANT PROFILE

HEIGHT 7m (22ft)

SPREAD 3m (10ft)

SITE Full sun or partial shade

SOIL Moist, fertile

HARDINESS Fully hardy

FLOWERING Midsummer to late autumn

Clematis cirrhosa 'Freckles'

C

THIS WINTER-BLOOMING, CLIMBING EVERGREEN can start flowering sporadically in late autumn, with a few flowers still showing in the spring. The flowers are creamy-pink with brownish-red spots and are slightly scented, while the leaves are finely cut, with a bronze tinge in the autumn. It needs a sheltered sunny site against a wall, where it can be fully appreciated. Plant it with its roots in shaded, moist, rich soil and with its head in the sun. Prune immediately after flowering, if required, to restrict its size.

OTHER VARIETY *C. montana* (very vigorous, white flowers with yellow centres).

PLANT PROFILE	
HEIGHT 3m (10ft)	
SPREAD 1.5m (5ft)	
SITE Full sun	
SOIL Moist, fertile	
HARDINESS Frost hardy	
FLOWERING Mid- or late winter	

C

Clematis macropetala 'Markham's Pink'

WITH EYE-CATCHING COLOURS from soft pink to rosy-mauve, this Chinese deciduous climber has 10cm (4in) wide flowers and, almost equally attractive, fluffy seedheads in the autumn. Gardener, poet and novelist Vita Sackville-West famously grew it out of an Ali Baba jar with a blue *Clematis macropetala*. It is perfectly hardy and tolerates exposed sites, but prefers its roots in shaded, moist, rich soil while the flowers should be in the sun. After flowering, remove dead and weak stems, and cut back the others only to keep it in check.

OTHER VARIETIES *C. cirrhosa* var. *balearica* (pale cream flowers with reddish-brown speckles); *C. montana* var. *rubens* (pink flowers, purple-flushed, mid-green leaves).

PLANT PROFILE
HEIGHT 3m (10ft)
SPREAD 1.5m (5ft)
SITE Full sun, partial shade
SOIL Moist, fertile
HARDINESS Fully hardy
FLOWERING Spring to early summer

Clematis montana f. grandiflora

C

A VIGOROUS, DECIDUOUS CLEMATIS, this is one of the best climbers for training through a tall tree or over a large wall or shed. It has a two-week flowering period when the white, 8cm (3in) wide flowers are an incredible sight. If it is being grown with another clematis, choose one that flowers in midsummer to carry on the show. When growing it through a tree, pruning is not necessary, but if it becomes overgrown, cut it back immediately after flowering. Water well during dry periods in summer when it puts on new growth for the following year's flower display.

PLANT PROFILE

HEIGHT 10m (30ft)

SPREAD 4m (12ft)

SITE Full sun

SOIL Moist, fertile

HARDINESS Fully hardy

FLOWERING Late spring and early summer

C

Clematis 'Perle d'Azur'

FOR COVERING WALLS or growing over a pergola, this vigorous, free-flowering, azure-blue, deciduous clematis is perfect. You can even construct a sturdy wooden vertical frame in the border, with wires between, and allow it to climb up and produce a wall of blue. Since the 8cm (3in) wide flowers are on the lighter side of blue, they look darker in partial shade and paler in full sun. Prune in early spring to a strong bud, 20cm (8in) above ground level.

OTHER VARIETIES *C.* 'Comtesse de Bouchaud' (large, bright mauve-pink flowers); *C.* 'Ernest Markham' (vivid magenta flowers); *C.* 'Gipsy Queen' (violet-purple flowers with red centres); *C.* 'Hagley Hybrid' (pinkish-mauve flowers); *C.* 'Jackmanii' (dark purple flowers).

PLANT PROFILE	
HEIGHT 3m (10ft)	
SPREAD 1m (3ft)	
SITE Sun or partial shade	
SOIL Moist, fertile	
HARDINESS Fully hardy	
FLOWERING Midsummer to early autumn	

Clematis 'Proteus'

C

THE FIRST BATCH OF BLOOMS from this vigorous, summer-flowering climber are up to 20cm (8in) wide, making it one of the best double-flowered, rich pink clematis for this time of year. In the second half of summer, the equally prolific second flush are single and smaller, up to 15cm (6in) wide. The colour can look rather washed out in full sun, and it should be planted in light shade, with the roots in moist, rich soil. Prune out dead and spindly stems in early spring, and reduce the rest to a healthy bud.

OTHER VARIETIES *C.* 'Beauty of Worcester' (deep blue flowers with white centres); *C.* 'Jackmanii Alba' (blue-tinged flowers with brown centres); *C.* 'Vyvyan Pennell' (lilac flowers with golden-yellow centres).

PLANT PROFILE
HEIGHT 3m (10ft)
SPREAD 1m (3ft)
SITE Full sun or semi-shade
SOIL Moist, fertile
HARDINESS Fully hardy
FLOWERING Mid-to late summer

C

Clematis rehderiana

VIGOROUS, FREE-FLOWERING AND DECIDUOUS, this clematis is ideal for sending up a large tree where it will produce a creamy-yellow show in the upper branches throughout the second half of summer and into autumn. During very dry spells in early summer, make sure that it is well watered to prevent stress. It needs to be planted in shaded, moist, rich soil where the flowers will receive plenty of sun. Vigorous climbers like this do not need much pruning if growing up a tree, but for flowers lower down the stems, cut it back in spring to 20cm (8in) above ground level.

OTHER VARIETIES *C. flammula* (white flowers); *C. integrifolia* (blue flowers); *C. tangutica* (yellow flowers, fluffy seedheads).

PLANT PROFILE

HEIGHT 7m (22ft)

SPREAD 3m (10ft)

SITE Sun or partial shade

SOIL Moist, fertile

HARDINESS Fully hardy

FLOWERING Midsummer to late autumn

Clematis viticella 'Purpurea Plena Elegans'

WITH ITS PURPLE-PINK DOUBLE FLOWERS, this is one of the best viticellas, and it can be grown up through other sturdy climbers, such as roses, using them as support. Alternatively, grow it over a pergola or through a large shrub. The roots need to be in shaded, moist, rich soil while the flowers are in the sun. Prune back to 20cm (8in) above the ground in early spring, and mulch with compost in late winter after a night of rain to lock moisture in the ground. Make sure that the mulch is not in contact with the plant's stems.

OTHER VARIETIES C. 'Etoile Violette' (violet-purple flowers); C. 'Madame Julia Correvon' (wine-red flowers); C. 'Niobe' (deep red flowers); C. 'Rouge Cardinal' (crimson flowers).

PLANT PROFILE

HEIGHT 3m (10ft)

SPREAD 1m (3ft)

SITE Sun or partial shade

SOIL Moist, fertile

HARDINESS Fully hardy

FLOWERING Midsummer to late autumn

Suckers growing around a shrub should be cut off where they meet the root; for new plants, remove them with a few roots intact and replant them.

C | *Clerodendrum trichotomum*

THIS SPECTACULAR, END-OF-SUMMER deciduous shrub or small tree for a woodland garden will struggle in cold winds and, as a result, grow slowly. In such conditions it could take six years to reach a height of 2m (6ft) and flower. It is vital, therefore, that you plant it in a sunny, sheltered position in free-draining soil where it will reward you in late summer with masses of small, star-like flowers with a scent similar to jasmine. The flowers are followed by eye-catching blue berries, each set in a red cup, which keep the show going well into autumn. Prune it for shape in early spring.

OTHER VARIETIES *C. bungei* (fragrant, dark pink flowers, young leaves tinged purple); *C. trichotomum* var. *fargesii* (bronze young leaves).

PLANT PROFILE

HEIGHT 6m (20ft)

SPREAD 6m (20ft)

SITE Full sun

SOIL Fertile, free-draining

HARDINESS Fully hardy

FLOWERING Late summer to mid-autumn

Clethra alnifolia Sweet pepper bush

TYPICALLY FOUND IN WOODLAND GARDENS, this deciduous, upright shrub must be grown in rich, free-draining, acid soil in order to thrive. The leaves are 10cm (4in) long, and in summer it produces spikes of tiny white flowers with a sweet, gentle scent. Every few years, prune back some of the old wood to near ground level which will clear the way for replacement stems to come through. You can also prune in late winter, removing any dead or damaged wood, to create an open network of stems.

OTHER VARIETIES *C. barbinervis* (white flowers, leaves turn red and yellow in autumn, peeling bark when mature); *C. delavayi* (white flowers from pink buds, blue-green leaves).

PLANT PROFILE
HEIGHT 2.5m (8ft)
SPREAD 2.5m (8ft)
SITE Partial or dappled shade
SOIL Acid, fertile, free-draining
HARDINESS Fully hardy
FLOWERING Late summer and early autumn

C | *Clianthus puniceus* Lobster claw

THIS IS A FUN, EVERGREEN SHRUB that features quirky, bright red flowers, thought by some to look like lobster's claws (the plant is also sometimes commonly known as parrot's bill). It is quite fussy in its growing requirements, needing a sunny, sheltered site, preferably against a protective wall for support. Plant it in average, free-draining soil – standing in cold, wet ground throughout winter will prove lethal – and apply a thick mulch of compost in autumn to protect it. If the top growth is cut back by frost, new shoots will, in most cases, emerge from the ground the following spring.

OTHER VARIETIES *C. puniceus* 'Albus' (white flowers flushed green); *C. puniceus* 'Roseus' (dark rose-pink flowers).

PLANT PROFILE

HEIGHT 4m (12ft)

SPREAD 3m (10ft)

SITE Full sun

SOIL Average, free-draining

HARDINESS Frost hardy

FLOWERING Spring to early summer

Cobaea scandens Cathedral bell

C

SPECTACULAR AND INCREDIBLY VIGOROUS, this tender climber is easily capable of sprinting up to 5m (15ft) in a single summer, when it produces fleshy, bell-shaped flowers about 5cm (2in) wide. Choose the planting site with care because once the stems take off, they will latch onto anything within reach. Give it a clear run up a sunny trellis, for example, or a fence or wall with horizontal wires firmly attached to act as supports. In hot summers, the flowers will be followed by egg-shaped, inedible, greenish-coloured fruit. Provide moist but free-draining, average soil, and grow it as an annual because it will not survive low temperatures.

PLANT PROFILE

HEIGHT 10–20m (30–70ft)

SITE Full sun

SOIL Moist but free-draining

HARDINESS Frost tender

FLOWERING Summer to autumn

C Codonopsis clematidea

THIS FIRST-RATE, TWINING PERENNIAL climber never gets out of hand, and produces a show of beautiful bell-shaped flowers. In the spring, fragile, easily broken stems emerge from the ground, and later the round buds open to reveal nodding pale blue flowers with a blue circular ring and yellow and black markings inside. Plant it where the flowers enjoy full sun and the roots cool, moist shade. It also needs protection against damaging winds, and take precautions against slugs and snails which can quickly devour the thin stems.

OTHER VARIETIES *C. convolvulacea* (violet-blue flowers); *C. lanceolata* (mauve-flushed, greeny-white flowers); *C. ovata* (greenish-blue flowers).

PLANT PROFILE

HEIGHT 5m (15ft)

SITE Sun or partial shade

SOIL Moist

HARDINESS Fully hardy

FLOWERING Late summer

Colletia paradoxa

C

THIS SOUTH AMERICAN SHRUB is both a beauty and a beast. It has pretty, almond-scented, creamy-white flowers, but also produces the most lethal green spines – large, stiff and triangular. It is a strange shrub in other respects because it hardly has any leaves. An architectural plant with a difference, it could be used as a secure, barbed-wire barrier for your garden boundary. Because it is not totally hardy, plant it in a sunny, sheltered site in soil with excellent drainage. A thick winter mulch of compost is also necessary in cold areas. If you want an even bushier, spinier plant, pinch out the growing tips when they are young.

OTHER VARIETY *C. hystrix* (tubular, fragrant, white flowers).

PLANT PROFILE	
HEIGHT 3m (10ft)	
SPREAD 5m (15ft)	
SITE Full sun	
SOIL Free-draining	
HARDINESS Frost hardy	
FLOWERING Autumn	

C | *Colquhounia coccinea*

USUALLY EVERGREEN, EXCEPT IN COLD WINTERS, this plant has two
chief assets. In addition to its 20cm (8in) long, pointed leaves that
are aromatic when crushed, it also produces bright orange to scarlet
flowers on short spikes. A highly desirable shrub, it cannot be grown
in an exposed, frosty garden, and to flourish needs a sunny, sheltered
position in average, free-draining soil. If the top growth is cut back
by a light frost, new shoots should emerge from ground level the
following spring. Where grown in a frost-free area during winter,
you should prune it hard to the bottom framework of stems in the
spring which will stimulate fresh, new growth.

PLANT PROFILE	
HEIGHT	2.5m (8ft)
SPREAD	2.5m (8ft)
SITE	Full sun
SOIL	Average, free-draining
HARDINESS	Frost hardy
FLOWERING	Late summer

Colutea arborescens Bladder senna

C

THE COMMON NAME of this deciduous shrub describes the unusual shape of its large seed pods, which look like bladders or kidney beans when seen from a distance. The pods ping open in autumn, flinging out the seed in all directions. During the summer it is bushy and quite eye-catching, with clusters of 2cm (¾in) long yellow flowers and attractive, divided, pale green leaves. It will grow well in average, free-draining soil, and should be pruned in early spring when you can cut it back to maintain its shape.

OTHER VARIETY *C. x media* (orange-brown flowers, greenish-brown pods); *C. orientalis* (smaller-growing, copper-red flowers, bluish-green leaves, pale brown pods).

PLANT PROFILE
HEIGHT 3m (10ft)
SPREAD 3m (10ft)
SITE Full sun
SOIL Average, free-draining
HARDINESS Fully hardy
FLOWERING Summer

C

Convolvulus cneorum

FOR A GAP AT THE FRONT OF A BORDER, this is an excellent choice of evergreen shrub. It will flower, from pink buds, throughout the summer – the open, trumpet-shaped, yellow-centred, white blooms standing out well against the silky, silver-green leaves. The flowers also contrast well with crimson and blue blooms. The oval-shaped plants perform best in moderately fertile, or even poor soil, and they also require good drainage and wall-to-wall sun. In areas with heavy, cold, wet winter soil, it is best to plant them in containers of gritty compost which can be positioned in a sheltered spot over winter.

OTHER VARIETY *C. sabatius* (pale to deep lavender-blue flowers).

PLANT PROFILE
HEIGHT 60cm (24in)
SPREAD 90cm (36in)
SITE Full sun
SOIL Free-draining
HARDINESS Frost hardy
FLOWERING Late spring to summer

Cornus alba 'Sibirica' Red-barked dogwood

C

THIS SUPERB DECIDUOUS SHRUB offers one of the best shows in the winter garden. It has striking, bright red, new stems which sprout out of the ground like the spines of a giant porcupine and retain their colour for a year or two. Prune every spring, or every other year, to just above ground level to force up new coloured growth (at the expense of any flowers). In large gardens these dogwoods are best planted in groups. 'Sibirica' tolerates a wide range of soils, including heavy clay, and for blazing stems, grow it in full sun.

OTHER VARIETIES *C. alba* 'Aurea' (yellow leaves, red stems); *C. alba* 'Elegantissima' (variegated foliage, red stems); *C. alba* 'Kesselringii' (blackish-purple winter shoots, red and purple leaves in autumn).

PLANT PROFILE
HEIGHT 2.5m (8ft)
SPREAD 2.5m (8ft)
SITE Full sun
SOIL Fertile, free-draining
HARDINESS Fully hardy
FLOWERING Late spring and early summer

C | *Cornus mas* Cornelian cherry

WITH CLUSTERS OF SMALL YELLOW FLOWERS which appear before
the leaves, this shrub is a bright choice for a winter garden. The
foliage flares up reddish-purple in the autumn before falling, when
bright red berries also form. It thrives in most soils, except extremes
of wet and dry, and pruning in early summer is necessary only to
keep it in shape. A smaller choice for medium-size gardens is the
2m (6ft) high *Cornus mas* 'Aureoelegantissima', the leaves of which
are edged with yellow and pink.

OTHER VARIETIES *C.* 'Ormonde' (purple and green flowers with
pink-tipped white bracts, leaves turn orange, red, or purple in autumn);
C. sanguinea 'Winter Beauty' (orange-yellow and red winter shoots).

PLANT PROFILE
HEIGHT 5m (15ft)
SPREAD 5m (15ft)
SITE Sun or partial shade
SOIL Moist but free-draining
HARDINESS Fully hardy
FLOWERING Late winter

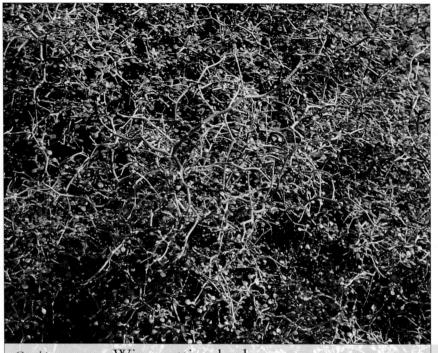

Corokia cotoneaster Wire-netting bush

C

THE HIGHLY APPROPRIATE COMMON NAME of this evergreen shrub comes from its stiff, wiry, tangled net of stems. Its curious, tiny leaves are spoon-shaped, and the small yellow flowers are gently scented and followed by bright red berries. None of the corokias is totally hardy, but *Corokia cotoneaster* is one of the toughest. Despite this, it still needs a sunny, sheltered position with free-draining, rich soil. A little gentle pruning may be necessary after flowering to maintain its shape, but it will tolerate harder pruning if required.

OTHER VARIETIES *C. x virgata* (fragrant yellow flowers followed by yellow or orange fruit); *C. x virgata* 'Bronze King' (dark bronze-tinged foliage); *C. x virgata* 'Yellow Wonder' (golden-yellow fruit).

PLANT PROFILE
HEIGHT 2.5m (8ft)
SPREAD 2.5m (8ft)
SITE Full sun
SOIL Fertile, free-draining
HARDINESS Frost hardy
FLOWERING Late spring

C *Coronilla valentina* subsp. *glauca* 'Variegata'

GIVEN THE RIGHT CONDITIONS, this extremely bushy, fruity-scented evergreen with cream-margined leaves will flower prolifically – not just once from late winter to early spring, but again in late summer. It requires a sunny position, shelter from cold winter winds and free-draining, average soil. The base of a south-facing wall is an ideal location or, without the right conditions, grow it in a conservatory. Pruning is not necessary, but if it becomes straggly and needs tidying up, cut it back in mid-spring and it will quickly reshoot.

OTHER VARIETIES   *C. valentina* subsp. *glauca* (smaller-growing, blue-green leaves); *C. valentina* subsp. *glauca* 'Citrina' (pale yellow flowers).

PLANT PROFILE	
HEIGHT 1.5m (5ft)	
SPREAD 1.5m (5ft)	
SITE Full sun	
SOIL Average, free-draining	
HARDINESS Frost hardy	
FLOWERING Late winter, early spring and summer	

Correa backhouseana Australian fuchsia

C

THE GOOD NEWS is that this native of southern Australia is capable of flowering right through the winter, but the bad news is that it needs a very sheltered, warm spot. The base of a sunny, protective wall is ideal as long as the soil is moist, rich and even slightly acidic. If outdoor conditions are not right, you can grow it in a border or large container in a conservatory or heated greenhouse where it should reliably produce 2.5cm (1in) long tubular, reddish-green or cream flowers, on a dense network of hairy, rust-red twigs.

OTHER VARIETIES *C.* 'Dusky Bells' (smaller-growing, dusky carmine-red flowers); *C.* 'Mannii' (red flowers); *C. reflexa* (green, white, pink, or red flowers, sometimes with green or cream petal tips).

PLANT PROFILE
HEIGHT 1–2m (3–6ft)
SPREAD 1.5–2.5m (5–8ft)
SITE Full sun
SOIL Moist, fertile
HARDINESS Half hardy
FLOWERING Late autumn to late spring

C | *Corylopsis pauciflora*

As ONE OF THE BEST SHRUBS for acid soil and light shade, *Corylopsis pauciflora* makes a thicket-like mass of twiggy growth that is covered in pale yellow flowers in the second half of spring. The blooms have a faint scent which is only detectable when you get up close. Almost maintenance free, pruning is unnecessary – if impossible, given its dense growth – but you can remove dead or damaged wood at any time of year. Good alternatives include the lemon-yellow *C. sinensis* var. *sinensis*, but it is not as hardy as *C. pauciflora*.

OTHER VARIETIES *C. glabrescens* (taller-growing, hanging clusters of pale yellow flowers, dark green leaves, blue-green beneath); *C. sinensis* var. *sinensis* 'Spring Purple' (dark plum-purple young leaves).

PLANT PROFILE

HEIGHT 1.5m (5ft)

SPREAD 1.5m (5ft)

SITE Partial shade

SOIL Acid, fertile, moist but free-draining

HARDINESS Fully hardy

FLOWERING Late spring

C

Corylus avellana 'Contorta' Corkscrew hazel

WITH TWISTY, CORKSCREW-LIKE bare branches, this deciduous shrub is a good choice for the winter garden. The branches make a lively architectural shape when viewed against the sky, and they are even more eye-catching at the end of winter when pale yellow, dangling catkins appear which are well worth including as part of an indoor arrangement. Most soils are fine, as long as they are free-draining and fertile. Pruning is not necessary, but remove any straight stems and prune to thin it out or for size in late winter.

OTHER VARIETIES *C. avellana* (broadly heart-shaped, round-tipped leaves, yellow catkins); *C. avellana* 'Aurea' (bright yellow young leaves).

PLANT PROFILE
HEIGHT 5m (15ft)
SPREAD 5m (15ft)
SITE Full sun or semi-shade
SOIL Fertile, free-draining
HARDINESS Fully hardy
FLOWERING Late winter and early spring

C

Corylus maxima 'Purpurea' Filbert

THIS IS AN EXCELLENT HAZEL to grow for its edible autumn nuts, late winter purple-tinged catkins, and young, rich purple foliage in spring which gradually darkens throughout the summer. 'Purpurea' does not have the unusual branches of the corkscrew hazel (*Corylus avellana* 'Contorta'), but it does grow a little taller, and is equally unfussy about its growing conditions, needing soil with very good drainage more than anything else. Its purple-tinged catkins also make a beautiful contribution to cut-flower arrangements.

OTHER VARIETIES *C. avellana* (yellow catkins in late winter); *C. avellana* 'Aurea' (bright yellow young leaves).

PLANT PROFILE

HEIGHT 6m (20ft)

SPREAD 5m (15ft)

SITE Full sun or partial shade

SOIL Free-draining

HARDINESS Fully hardy

FLOWERING Late winter

Cotinus coggygria Smoke bush

C

INJECTING INTEREST INTO AN AUTUMN BORDER, the leaves of this bushy deciduous shrub turn arresting shades of red and yellow before they fall. Its common name describes the tiny flowers on its mature stems which produce a blurred, smoky effect throughout the summer. For the best flowers and leaf colour, it needs average soil that is neither too moist nor over-rich, and a long hot summer. It is a first-rate plant but does require space, although it can be pruned in early spring to restrict its size and remove dead wood.

OTHER VARIETIES *C. coggygria* 'Notcutt's Variety' (wine-red leaves, purple-pink flowers); *C. coggygria* 'Royal Purple' (dark purple foliage); *C.* 'Flame' (orange-red autumn tints); *C.* 'Grace' (bright red autumn tints).

PLANT PROFILE
HEIGHT 5m (15ft)
SPREAD 5m (15ft)
SITE Full sun or partial shade
SOIL Average, free-draining
HARDINESS Fully hardy
FLOWERING Summer

C

Cotoneaster horizontalis

THE BEST REASON for growing this plant is its fishbone-like stems which are covered with scarlet berries in autumn and into winter, if the birds leave them alone. Other attractions include the deciduous red autumn leaves, white pink-tinged flowers in the spring, and its ability to grow on shady walls. Like all cotoneasters, it tolerates most soils but avoid soaking wet ground and overfeeding. Prune in late winter to accentuate its shape.

OTHER VARIETIES *C. adpressus* (shorter-growing, red-tinged white flowers, bright red fruit); *C. conspicuus* (evergreen, white flowers, red fruit); *C.* 'Hybridus Pendulus' (taller-growing, white flowers, red fruit); *C. procumbens* (green leaves purplish when young).

PLANT PROFILE
HEIGHT 1m (3ft)
SPREAD 1.5m (5ft)
SITE Full sun but shade tolerant
SOIL Average, free-draining
HARDINESS Fully hardy
FLOWERING Late spring

Cotoneaster 'Rothschildianus'

THE ARCHING STEMS of this semi-evergreen to evergreen shrub are covered in long, thin, pale green leaves. There is a good show of whitish flowers at the start of summer, followed by butter-yellow berries that hang on into winter. An excellent partner for a red-berried cotoneaster in a shrub border, you can also grow it as a hedge or at the edge of a wooded area of the garden. Like all cotoneasters, it tolerates most soils, but avoid soaking wet or very fertile ground.

OTHER VARIETIES *C. franchettii* (smaller-growing, red-flushed white flowers, orange-red fruit); *C. lacteus* (green leaves, white-felted beneath, milky-white flowers, red fruit); *C. salicifolius* (white flowers, red fruit).

PLANT PROFILE	
HEIGHT 5m (15ft)	
SPREAD 5m (15ft)	
SITE Sun or partial shade	
SOIL Average, free-draining	
HARDINESS Fully hardy	
FLOWERING Early summer	

C | *Crinodendron hookerianum* Lantern tree

TYPICALLY A LARGE EVERGREEN SHRUB, or possibly a small tree in the right conditions, this Chilean plant has downward-pointing flowers that look like miniature lanterns or tulips. Although flower buds appear in the autumn, they do not begin to fatten until the spring, opening right at the end of that season. The lantern tree is slightly fussy, needing a sheltered site to avoid leaf scorch, and the roots must be in cool, moist, shaded, acid soil. When provided with these conditions, it will reward you with an impressive show. Any pruning necessary to maintain shape should be done after flowering.

OTHER VARIETY *C. patagua* (scented, white fringed flowers).

PLANT PROFILE
HEIGHT 4m (12ft) after 12 years
SPREAD 2.5m (8ft) after 12 years
SITE Full sun to partial shade
SOIL Acid, moist
HARDINESS Frost hardy
FLOWERING All summer

Cytisus battandieri Pineapple broom

C

THE BRIGHT YELLOW FLOWERS of this deciduous tree-like shrub are up to 15cm (6in) long and smell of freshly cut pineapples, which accounts for its common name. The silvery leaves can be 10cm (4in) long. It generally thrives best against a sunny, sheltered wall, although you can grow it in a protected border. It dislikes being moved once it is in the ground, and requires free-draining, poor, acid soil – wet, heavy ground will prove fatal.

OTHER VARIETIES   *C.* 'Burkwoodii' (dark pink flowers with yellow margins); *C. x kewensis* (cream flowers); *C. multiflorus* (white flowers); *C.* 'Zeelandia' (creamy-white and lilac-pink flowers).

PLANT PROFILE
HEIGHT 5m (15ft)
SPREAD 5m (15ft)
SITE Full sun
SOIL Acid, poor, free-draining
HARDINESS Frost hardy
FLOWERING Mid- and late summer

C   *Cytisus* x *praecox* 'Allgold' Broom

ONE OF THE PARENTS of this attractive broom is dense and bushy, while the other is incredibly free-flowering: put them together and they produce this deciduous, compact shrub which has long-lasting, dark yellow flowers. It is easy to grow, needing average garden soil which can be poor and acid. Prune it after flowering for shape, if necessary, but don't cut back into the old wood – the less 'Allgold' is pruned, the better the flowering will be.

OTHER VARIETIES *C.* 'Boskoop Ruby' (red flowers); *C.* 'Hollandia' (cream and dark pink flowers); *C.* 'Lena' (dark yellow flowers with bright red wings).

PLANT PROFILE
HEIGHT 1.2m (4ft)
SPREAD 1.5m (5ft)
SITE Full sun
SOIL Average
HARDINESS Fully hardy
FLOWERING Mid- and late spring

Daboecia cantabrica subsp. *scotica* 'William Buchanan'

D

THIS DWARF SHRUB is suitable for acid soil and is a good choice for the front of a border, as it flowers reliably throughout the growing season. It can also be grown in rock gardens or raised beds, and needs to be in a sheltered position. The brightly coloured flowers are borne well clear of the evergreen leaves. The pruning regime could not be simpler – a light, all-over trim in the spring to remove last year's dead flower stalks, thus keeping the plant neat and smart. If you grow two or three different kinds together you can create a patchwork quilt of colours.

OTHER VARIETIES *D. cantabrica* 'Bicolor' (flowers in white, pink and beetroot red); *D. cantabrica* subsp. *scotica* 'Silverwells' (white flowers).

PLANT PROFILE	
HEIGHT 35cm (14in)	
SPREAD 55cm (22in)	
SITE Full sun	
SOIL Free-draining	
HARDINESS Frost hardy	
FLOWERING Late spring to mid-autumn	

D | *Danae racemosa* Alexandrian laurel

A BIT OF A BOTANICAL CURIOSITY, the leaves of this unusual, compact, slow-growing evergreen shrub from woodland regions in Turkey are, in fact, flat branches. At the start of the summer, small, greenish-yellow flowers appear, and these are followed by tiny, glossy red or orange-red berries that make more impact than the blooms. Both the unusual branches and the bright berries are suitable for a cut-flower display. For the best results, grow Alexandrian laurel in rich, moist but free-draining soil, and choose a position where it has shelter from strong, damaging winds. Cut old stems right back in the spring before the new season's growth gets under way.

PLANT PROFILE

HEIGHT 1m (3ft)

SPREAD 1m (3ft)

SITE Sun or shade

SOIL Fertile, moist but free-draining

HARDINESS Frost hardy

FLOWERING Early summer

Daphne mezereum

D

THE FABULOUS SCENT from tiny flowers at the top of bare stems in late winter and early spring is the main attraction. In exposed and cold areas, provide a sunny, sheltered spot where the scent will linger. It thrives on chalk but is quite happy on many different types of soil, provided it is moist but free-draining and reasonably fertile – the roots must not dry out or become waterlogged. Don't be put off by its reputation for being tricky to grow, but do note that the sap can be an irritant and that all parts are toxic if eaten.

OTHER VARIETIES *D. bholua* var. *glacialis* 'Gurkha' (white flowers flushed purple-pink, blackish-purple fruit); *D. cneorum* 'Eximia' (shorter-growing, rose-pink flowers from crimson buds).

PLANT PROFILE
HEIGHT 1.2m (4ft)
SPREAD 1m (3ft)
SITE Full sun or light shade
SOIL Moist but free-draining
HARDINESS Fully hardy
FLOWERING Late winter and early spring

D

Decaisnea fargesii

THIS DECIDUOUS, UPRIGHT CHINESE SHRUB has three quirky features that make it very popular. First, after flowering it produces 10cm (4in) long seed pods that look like metallic-blue broad beans. Second, the drooping, bell-shaped, green or yellow-green, early summer flowers do not actually have any petals. Third, the leaves are up to 90cm (36in) long and consist of up to 25 leaflets that turn an attractive yellow in the autumn. It is easy to grow, given the right conditions – rich, moist but free-draining soil, and shelter from strong winds. A position in a wooded area of the garden provides the necessary shelter.

PLANT PROFILE

HEIGHT 6m (20ft)

SPREAD 6m (20ft)

SITE Sun or partial shade

SOIL Fertile, moist but free-draining

HARDINESS Fully hardy

FLOWERING Early summer

Dendromecon rigida Tree poppy

D

IN ITS NATIVE CALIFORNIA, the tree poppy grows in full sun on dry, rocky slopes which is why it needs a warm, sheltered spot to thrive in the garden. Choose a planting position with free-draining soil – perhaps in a gravel garden, on top of a bank, or at the foot of a wall – where it will produce blue-green, willow-like leaves, and bright yellow, poppy-like, gently scented flowers. When it is being wall-trained, cut back the flowered stems in summer after flowering to just 2–4 buds from the main framework. If growing it as a bush, in early spring cut back winter-damaged or weak stems to a healthy, outward-facing bud. It can be grown close to *Fremontodendron* 'California Glory' which enjoys the same conditions.

PLANT PROFILE	
HEIGHT 3m (10ft)	
SPREAD 3m (10ft)	
SITE Full sun	
SOIL Free-draining	
HARDINESS Frost hardy	
FLOWERING Spring to autumn	

D | *Desfontainia spinosa*

FOR GARDENS WITH ACID OR NEUTRAL SOIL, this dramatic South American plant is ideal. It produces showy, red, tubular flowers with yellow tips and makes a medium-size, slow-growing evergreen bush with shiny, holly-like leaves. You can prolong the flowering period by keeping the soil moist with a thick mulch of compost, which should be applied in the spring after a downpour. It is not totally hardy and needs a protected, sheltered site – for example, at the foot of a wall where it will receive shade in the middle of the day. Pruning is rarely needed, but you can give it a light trim in spring for shape. If it is not looking happy in its position, keep trying it in different places because, when it does thrive, it is a marvellous shrub.

PLANT PROFILE

HEIGHT 2m (6ft)

SPREAD 2m (6ft)

SITE Dappled shade

SOIL Moist

HARDINESS Frost hardy

FLOWERING Midsummer to late autumn

Desmodium elegans

D

THIS SUBTLE, UNASSUMING SHRUB really comes into its own at the end of the growing season, when many other garden plants are beginning to look a little tired and past their best. The large, 25cm (10in) long leaves consist of three leaflets, and they are joined by airy sprays, about 20cm (8in) long, of tiny lilac to deep pink flowers. The stems should be cut back in the spring in order to force up strong, new growth. *Desmodium elegans* is not completely hardy and to thrive requires free-draining soil and a warm, sheltered position.

OTHER VARIETY *D. yunnanense* (taller-growing, clusters of pea-like, purple flowers, pale green downy leaves).

PLANT PROFILE	
HEIGHT 1.5m (5ft)	
SPREAD 1.5m (5ft)	
SITE Full sun	
SOIL Free-draining	
HARDINESS Frost hardy	
FLOWERING Late summer to autumn	

D

Deutzia x *hybrida* 'Mont Rose'

ERECT, DENSE AND VIGOROUS, this is a medium-high, deciduous shrub with arching stems of five-petalled, purple-pink blooms set against dark green foliage. A beautiful plant for a border, it is also extremely easy to grow and will tolerate most soils, but don't let the ground dry out in the summer. To avoid this, add a thick mulch of compost around the plant, avoiding the stems, in the spring after a night of heavy rain to help lock moisture in the ground. There are also many excellent spring- and summer-flowering alternatives.

OTHER VARIETIES *D. compacta* 'Lavender Time' (taller-growing, lilac flowers fading with age); *D.* x *kalmiiflora* (taller-growing, star-shaped, deep pink flowers).

PLANT PROFILE	
HEIGHT 1.2m (4ft)	
SPREAD 1.2m (4ft)	
SITE Full sun or light shade	
SOIL Moist but free-draining	
HARDINESS Fully hardy	
FLOWERING Early summer	

Dipelta floribunda

D

SWEETLY SCENTED, TUBULAR FLOWERS, opening at the end of spring, make this substantial deciduous shrub a real garden asset. It is multi-stemmed and open-looking with thin, peeling bark and beautiful, 10cm (4in) long, pointed leaves. It grows in rich, free-draining soil, and will flourish in chalky, alkaline conditions. After the pale pink flowers are over, prune the flowered stems back to strong buds. You can remove one-quarter of the old stems of established plants right back to the base every few years to encourage new growth, and to keep an open framework of branches.

OTHER VARIETY *D. yunnanensis* (smaller-growing, white flowers with orange markings).

PLANT PROFILE
HEIGHT 4m (12ft)
SPREAD 4m (12ft)
SITE Sun or partial shade
SOIL Fertile, free-draining
HARDINESS Fully hardy
FLOWERING Late spring and early summer

D

Disanthus cercidifolius

FOUND GROWING IN WOODLAND AND MOUNTAINOUS regions of China and Japan, this decorative deciduous shrub is highly rated for the autumn garden. Its blue–green leaves turn flamboyant shades of red, orange, and purple at the end of the year, with all colours on show at the same time. In addition, you have the bonus of faintly scented, spidery, rose-red flowers which also appear in autumn. Given its modest size, and that it can be grown as a showy boundary plant, it deserves to be far more popular than it is. Although completely hardy, make sure you provide it with a sheltered position where it will be protected from destructive strong winds.

PLANT PROFILE

HEIGHT 3m (10ft)

SPREAD 3m (10ft)

SITE Full sun

SOIL Moist, free-draining

HARDINESS Fully hardy

FLOWERING Mid-autumn

Dodonaea viscosa 'Purpurea' Hop bush

D

THE FLOWERS ON THIS SPREADING, evergreen, Australian shrub or small tree are quite insignificant, but the winged seed capsules in the summer and autumn put on a far better show, and come in shades ranging from pink to reddish-brown, light brown, purple, and yellow. The leaves are equally attractive, with a strong purplish-red hue. Young plants, especially if you are growing them as a temporary hedge, ought to have their growing tips pinched out to make them bushier and to give a better show of coloured foliage. Grow the hop bush in moist but free-draining soil in a protected, sunny spot in summer, but bring it indoors as soon as the temperatures start to plummet in late autumn as it is not hardy.

PLANT PROFILE

HEIGHT 1–5m (3–15ft)

SPREAD 1–3m (3–10ft)

SITE Full sun

SOIL Moist, fertile, free-draining

HARDINESS Half hardy

FLOWERING Early summer

D

Dregea sinensis

THIS DECIDUOUS, SCENTED, TWINING, Chinese climber is usually grown in conservatories, but it can easily be grown outside if you are prepared to pamper it a little. It needs the protection of a hot, sunny wall (with horizontal wires for it to climb up), shelter from the wind and free-draining soil. It could also be grown over an arch outside a front or back door. The leaves are small and heart-shaped, while the clusters of tiny pink flowers that open in summer are gently scented – the perfume is more intense in a warm, windless position. Grow this climber in free-draining soil and, if space is limited, prune it in spring. Provide a protective mulch of compost over the soil, leaving the stem area clear, in the autumn.

PLANT PROFILE

HEIGHT 3m (10ft)

SITE Sun or partial shade

SOIL Free-draining

HARDINESS Frost hardy

FLOWERING Summer

Drimys lanceolata Mountain pepper

D

UPRIGHT AND EVERGREEN, this shrub peaks in spring when scores of small, white flowers open. If you have separate male and female shrubs, these flowers will be followed by small, dark red or black berries. Mountain pepper also has reddish young stems and shiny, scented leaves. An Australian native, it requires a degree of wind and frost protection over the winter, while the soil should be fertile, and moist but free-draining. Pruning is rarely necessary, but unwanted or wayward stems can be removed after flowering.

OTHER VARIETY *D. winteri* (taller-growing, aromatic bark, large clusters of fragrant, ivory-white flowers).

PLANT PROFILE
HEIGHT 4m (12ft)
SPREAD 2.5m (8ft)
SITE Sun or partial shade
SOIL Fertile, moist but free-draining
HARDINESS Frost hardy
FLOWERING Mid- and late spring

E

Eccremocarpus scaber Chilean glory flower

THIS SPECTACULAR EVERGREEN climber from South America has small, bright, brash tubular flowers. It will survive colder climates for a few years if provided with a sunny, sheltered position, but you will eventually have to replace it. It can also be grown from seed and will shoot up 2.5m (8ft) or more and flower in its first summer. If caught by a frost, however, the stems die but new growth should appear in the following spring if given a winter mulch of compost. The soil should be on the light side, free-draining, and fertile. It can be pruned in spring if it has grown too large, although in cold areas it may well get cut back by the frost anyway.

OTHER VARIETY *E. scaber carmineus* (carmine-red flowers).

PLANT PROFILE	
HEIGHT To 5m (15ft)	
SITE Full sun	
SOIL Fertile, free-draining	
HARDINESS Frost hardy	
FLOWERING Late spring to autumn	

Elaeagnus x *ebbingei* 'Gilt Edge'

E

DARK GREEN LEAVES with eye-catching yellow margins are this fast-growing evergreen's most striking feature. It makes a good backdrop for a mixed or shrub border, or you could grow it as hedging or a windbreak in a coastal garden. The more sun it gets, the better the display of autumn flowers which, although insignificant to look at, produce a wonderful, fruity scent. Grow it in free-draining, fertile soil, and prune in the spring to keep it shapely. Remove any all-green shoots to stop the plant eventually losing its variegation.

OTHER VARIETIES *E. angustifolia* (red-tinted branches, flowers followed by silvery-yellow fruit); *E.* x *ebbingei* 'Limelight' (silvery young leaves becoming marked with pale green and yellow).

PLANT PROFILE	
HEIGHT 4m (12ft)	
SPREAD 4m (12ft)	
SITE Full sun	
SOIL Fertile, free-draining	
HARDINESS Fully hardy	
FLOWERING Autumn	

E Elaeagnus 'Quicksilver'

HIGHLY RATED FOR ITS SILVER-GREY FOLIAGE, which is particularly bright in the spring, 'Quicksilver' is a fast-growing, open, deciduous shrub. The star-shaped yellow flowers open from silver buds in the summer. It can be grown as an individual focal point or as a lively foil for a wide range of other colours, from dark green to red, in a border or gravel garden. It will also grow quite happily in a windy coastal garden. Plant it in free-draining, fertile soil, but avoid chalk, and prune lightly in the spring to keep it smart and shapely.

OTHER VARIETIES *E. commutata* (red-brown shoots, leaves covered with silvery scales); *E. pungens* 'Maculata' (leaf centres boldly marked with dark yellow).

PLANT PROFILE

HEIGHT 4m (12ft)

SPREAD 4m (12ft)

SITE Full sun

SOIL Fertile, free-draining

HARDINESS Fully hardy

FLOWERING Summer

Eleutherococcus sieboldianus

E

THIS TALL-GROWING DECIDUOUS SHRUB can be grown as part of a garden perimeter due to its spiny, cane-like stems which make good hedging material. It has large, hand-shaped leaves consisting of smaller leaflets, and small, star-shaped, greenish-white flowers that appear from late spring. These are followed by tiny black berries. It thrives in poor, dry, free-draining soil. Don't try growing this shrub on heavy clay soil that stays wet in winter because these conditions will quickly kill it.

OTHER VARIETY *E. sieboldianus* 'Variegatus' (leaves margined with creamy-white).

PLANT PROFILE	
HEIGHT	2.5m (8ft)
SPREAD	2.5m (8ft)
SITE	Full sun
SOIL	Dry, free-draining
HARDINESS	Fully hardy
FLOWERING	Late spring and early summer

E

Elsholtzia stauntonii

THIS AUTUMN-FLOWERING, deciduous shrub is well worth growing to add a touch of late-season colour. Its tiny purple-pink flowers are held on 15cm (6in) long candle-like spikes, while the equally long leaves give off a distinct smell of mint when torn, and turn red in the autumn before falling. It is slightly tender, and needs a sunny, sheltered position in the garden with rich, free-draining soil. In cold areas grow it in a pot and bring under cover for the winter. In spring, cut back all growth to the permanent framework of stems to force up new flowering wood.

OTHER VARIETY *E. stauntonii* 'Alba' (white flowers).

PLANT PROFILE

HEIGHT 1.5m (5ft)

SPREAD 1.5m (5ft)

SITE Full sun

SOIL Fertile, free-draining

HARDINESS Frost hardy

FLOWERING Late summer to autumn

Embothrium coccineum Chilean fire bush

E

GETTING THE SUMMER OFF to a lively start, this plant is a contender for any hot colour scheme. It produces a show of abundant flower clusters, and the scarlet (occasionally yellow) tubular blooms really stand out against a background of green, glossy leaves. Chilean fire bush has the added advantages of being quick-growing, evergreen (or semi-evergreen, depending on climate), and multi-branched. Plant it in rich, moist but free-draining soil that can be on the acid side, with some protection from the damaging effects of the wind.

OTHER VARIETY *E. coccineum* Lanceolatum Group 'Norquinco' (attractive narrowly lance-shaped leaves)

PLANT PROFILE
HEIGHT 10m (30ft)
SPREAD 5m (15ft)
SITE Full sun or partial shade
SOIL Moist, fertile, free-draining
HARDINESS Fully hardy
FLOWERING Late spring and early summer

E

Enkianthus campanulatus

IF YOU HAVE ACID SOIL, and space to spare, why not try this Japanese shrub which has heavy clusters of bell-like flowers with pink to red veining? The leaves add extra colours to the autumn garden with a show of orange-yellow, turning red, before falling. Either grow one as a feature plant where its rich autumn colours can be readily seen, or combine it with other late-season performers. It requires plenty of space and a site in full sun or partial shade, although growth is not as vigorous in shadier positions.

OTHER VARIETIES *E. cernuus* f. *rubens* (rich red flowers, leaves dark red-purple in autumn); *E. chinensis* (creamy-yellow flowers, leaves orange and red in autumn); *E. perulatus* (compact, smaller-growing).

PLANT PROFILE

HEIGHT 4–5m (12–15ft)

SPREAD 4–5m (12–15ft)

SITE Full sun or partial shade

SOIL Acid, moist but free-draining

HARDINESS Fully hardy

FLOWERING Late spring and early summer

Erica arborea var. *alpina* Tree heath

E

LIBERALLY COVERED IN DENSE CLUSTERS of white spring flowers, you can grow this excellent plant beside other tree heaths with blooms or leaves in contrasting shades. Unlike many ericas which are ground-hugging, spreading shrubs, this is a tall, upright plant. Ideally, you should grow it in acid, free-draining soil with well-rotted organic matter dug into it before planting. Prune after it has flowered in its first two or three years, cutting back stems by two-thirds, which will encourage bushier growth. In subsequent years, prune only to keep it neat and to cut out dead and diseased wood.

OTHER VARIETIES *E. arborea* 'Albert's Gold' (gold leaves); *E. carnea* 'Ann Sparkes' (pink flowers, gold leaves).

PLANT PROFILE
HEIGHT 2m (6ft)
SPREAD 85cm (34in)
SITE Full sun
SOIL Acid, free-draining
HARDINESS Fully hardy
FLOWERING Spring

E

Erica carnea 'Foxhollow' Winter heath

MOST WINTER HEATHS have white, pink, purple, or red flowers, and this pale pink type stands out because its yellow leaves turn orange-red when the temperatures drop. Choose carefully and you can have ericas in flower from midwinter to late spring, creating a carpet of colour when it is badly needed. In spring and summer, the spreading stems of evergreen leaves also block out the light and suppress weed growth. Winter heaths need acid, free-draining soil, and should be pruned after flowering, leaving 2.5cm (1in) of top-growth.

OTHER VARIETIES *E. carnea* 'Adrienne Duncan' (bronze foliage); *E. carnea* 'Challenger' (bold magenta flowers); *E. carnea* 'Golden Starlet' (white flowers, lime-green leaves).

PLANT PROFILE

HEIGHT 15cm (6in)

SPREAD 40cm (16in)

SITE Full sun

SOIL Free-draining

HARDINESS Fully hardy

FLOWERING Late winter and early spring

Erythrina crista-galli Cock's comb

E

THIS WOODY-STEMMED SOUTH AMERICAN plant produces bizarre,
rich red flowers toward the end of summer. These appear on stems
protected by long, fierce-looking spines, which means it must be
kept out of reach of children and away from paths. If you can
provide a sunny, sheltered position in your garden – for example,
against a warm wall – with rich, moist but free-draining soil, it
should succeed. Add a protective winter mulch of compost to be
safe. Cock's comb is definitely worth trying, not least for its glossy,
leathery leaves, and if the top-growth is cut back after a cold winter
new shoots should emerge at ground level the following spring. It
can also be grown in a large tub, and this allows you to bring it into
a conservatory over winter and take it outdoors once more for the
summer season.

PLANT PROFILE
HEIGHT 2.5m (8ft)
SPREAD 1.5m (5ft)
SITE Full sun
SOIL Moist, fertile, free-draining
HARDINESS Frost hardy
FLOWERING Late summer to autumn

E

Escallonia 'Apple Blossom'

THESE EXCELLENT, ALL-PURPOSE SHRUBS flower from the start of summer until the autumn, and when the weather is warm the shiny evergreen leaves also produce a gentle, sweet scent. Even better, this pretty plant tolerates coastal conditions where it can be used for hedging or a windbreak. Inland, however, it needs a more sheltered site that provides protection against frosts and icy winds. Escallonias thrive in well-drained soil, and if pruning is required to maintain their shape, do this immediately after flowering. In coastal gardens they may exceed 2.5m (8ft) in height and spread.

OTHER VARIETIES *E.* 'Donard Radiance' (rich pink flowers); *E.* 'Iveyi' (white flowers); *E. rubra* 'Crimson Spire' (crimson flowers).

PLANT PROFILE
HEIGHT 2.5m (8ft)
SPREAD 2.5m (8ft)
SITE Full sun
SOIL Free-draining
HARDINESS Frost hardy
FLOWERING Early and midsummer

HARD PRUNING

Pruning gum trees hard each year will restrict their size, and encourages more new, young stems with bright foliage to grow. In late spring, prune the previous year's stems back to within 5–8cm (2–3in) of the main trunk.

Eucalyptus pauciflora subsp. *niphophila* Snow gum

WITH WHITE BARK peeling off from mid-spring to autumn to reveal green, brownish-red and grey-coloured bark beneath, the snow gum is a beautiful garden plant. Although officially a tree, reaching up to 6m (20ft) in height, the snow gum can be pruned hard to keep it multi-stemmed and shrubby, and only about 3m (10ft) high. Start this pollarding process when the plant is three years old by cutting off the stems to a low framework in late spring. This encourages new growth and the attractive immature foliage, but as a result you may not get the full effect of the peeling bark.

OTHER VARIETIES   *E. gregsoniana* (white flowers, bluish-green young leaves); *E. nicholii* (reddish-brown bark, blue-green young leaves).

PLANT PROFILE

HEIGHT 3m (10ft)

SPREAD 3m (10ft)

SITE Full sun

SOIL Free-draining

HARDINESS Fully hardy

FLOWERING Early summer

E | *Eucryphia glutinosa*

THIS IS ONE OF THE BEST SHRUBS you can buy. It has toothed, glossy dark green leaves and in mild areas it is semi–evergreen. Growing to a substantial size, it could almost be called a small tree, and produces a lavish spread of white, sometimes double, 6cm (2½in) wide flowers that open in mid- to late summer. The leaves offer a further show of colour in the autumn when they redden as temperatures drop. This is the hardiest of the eucryphias, and does best when the roots are kept in the shade while the top is in the sun. Prune for shape, as necessary, in the spring.

PLANT PROFILE

HEIGHT	10m (30ft)
SPREAD	6m (20ft)
SITE	Full sun
SOIL	Moist, fertile, free-draining
HARDINESS	Fully hardy
FLOWERING	Mid- and late summer

Euonymus europaeus Spindle

E

MAKING ITS MARK IN THE AUTUMN, when scores of crimson, berry-like capsules split open to reveal tiny orange seeds within, this is an excellent deciduous shrub for free-draining soil, especially chalk. The leaves also colour up in the autumn, turning purple-red before falling. The wood is very hard, and was used for making spindles for spinning wheels – hence its common name. Plant it in sun to light up the autumn capsules, and prune in late winter. An excellent, tree-like alternative is 'Red Cascade', with scarlet autumn foliage.

OTHER VARIETIES *E. alatus* (leaves turn dark red in autumn, reddish-purple fruit); *E. japonicus* (white-tinged pink fruit); *E. latifolius* (leaves turn brilliant red in autumn, red fruit); *E. planipes* (red fruit).

PLANT PROFILE
HEIGHT 3m (10ft)
SPREAD 3m (10ft)
SITE Sun or semi-shade
SOIL Free-draining
HARDINESS Fully hardy
FLOWERING Late spring

E

Euonymus fortunei 'Silver Queen'

EACH LEAF OF THIS HARDY EVERGREEN has a band of white (pale yellow in the spring) around a dark green centre. For about 10 days it is covered in tiny greenish-white flowers, but a long hot summer is needed if berries are to be produced in any number. When grown against a wall it will turn into a self-clinging climber and shoot up to double its usual height. For good leaf colour, full sun is needed, and it will grow in most soils (except very wet). Prune immediately after flowering, when necessary, to control its size and shape.

OTHER VARIETIES *E. fortunei* 'Emerald Gaiety' (compact, white leaf margins turn pink in winter); *E. fortunei* 'Emerald 'n' Gold' (bright yellow leaf margins turn pink in winter).

PLANT PROFILE

HEIGHT 2.5m (8ft)

SPREAD 1.5m (5ft)

SITE Full sun or light shade

SOIL Free-draining

HARDINESS Fully hardy

FLOWERING Late spring or summer

In midsummer, prune back the flowered stems to a strong shoot or bud low down. Wash your hands after handling this plant as all parts are toxic.

Euphorbia characias subsp. *wulfenii*

E

DRAMATIC AND SHAPELY, this shrub has long, stiff, erect stems with finger-like, bluish-green leaves, while the flowers are made up of yellow-green, cup-like bracts and purple nectar glands. Grow it as a feature plant or in a large container, but it needs space to be fully appreciated. The soil must be light and free-draining, and give it a position where it receives protection from icy winds. Cut off the flowered shoots at the base in the summer after blooming and they will be replaced by new, flower-bearing stems the following spring.

OTHER VARIETIES *E. amygdaloides* var. *robbiae* (smaller-growing, reddish-green stems); *E. characias* subsp. *wulfenii* 'John Tomlinson' (almost spherical heads of yellow-green flowers).

PLANT PROFILE	
HEIGHT 1.2m (4ft)	
SPREAD 1.2m (4ft)	
SITE Full sun	
SOIL Free-draining	
HARDINESS Frost hardy	
FLOWERING Spring and early summer	

E

Euryops acraeus

DWARF AND EYE-CATCHING, this beautiful evergreen shrub produces a profusion of daisy-like, deep yellow flowers and makes a compact mound of silver-grey, leathery leaves. An ideal plant for a rock or gravel garden, it is also suitable for a border if given a position right at the front where it can be seen and appreciated. In its native South Africa it grows on mountain slopes where the soil is free-draining and not too fertile. It needs the same conditions in the garden; it will quickly weaken and die if the roots are locked in wet soil over winter. It will also benefit from some shelter against hard frosts because it is only just fully hardy.

OTHER VARIETY *E. pectinatus* (taller, bright yellow flowers).

PLANT PROFILE
HEIGHT 30cm (12in)
SPREAD 30cm (12in)
SITE Full sun
SOIL Free-draining
HARDINESS Fully hardy
FLOWERING Late spring and early summer

Exochorda x *macrantha* 'The Bride'

E

WITH A TERRIFIC DISPLAY OF FLOWERS lasting only about eight days, make sure you are at home at the start of summer. That is when this compact, deciduous shrub puts on an impressive show of pure white blooms held on arching stems. Slow growing – it puts on just 1m (3ft) of growth in five years – it makes an excellent choice for small gardens. It is also extremely reliable and thrives in most soils except for very wet or shallow, chalky ground. It is best planted with other shrubs that flower afterwards to keep a good show going throughout the summer months.

OTHER VARIETIES *E. giraldii* (taller-growing); *E. giraldii* var. *wilsonii* (white flowers, green-stalked leaves, pinkish-green when young).

PLANT PROFILE
HEIGHT 2m (6ft)
SPREAD 3m (10ft)
SITE Full sun or light dappled shade
SOIL Free-draining
HARDINESS Fully hardy
FLOWERING Late spring and early summer

F

Fabiana imbricata f. violacea

THIS BEAUTIFUL, MEDIUM-SIZED, evergreen shrub has upright stems and spreading, horizontal branches. It produces scores of small, white to pale mauve, tubular flowers nestling among the needle-like, green leaves, giving a fresh, bright, early summer show. Fabianas need a sunny, sheltered position in order to thrive – for example, at the foot of a wall – with free-draining, neutral to slightly acid soil. You can also grow it in a rock garden or right at the front of a border, but avoid planting it on thin soil over a chalk base.

OTHER VARIETIES *F. imbricata* (taller-growing); *F. imbricata* 'Prostrata' (low-growing, white flowers).

PLANT PROFILE
HEIGHT 1m (3ft)
SPREAD 2m (6ft)
SITE Full sun
SOIL Fertile, free-draining
HARDINESS Frost hardy
FLOWERING Early summer

Fallopia baldschuanica Russian vine

F

THIS IS A NO-NONSENSE, rampant, fast-spreading deciduous climber with clusters of white flowers in the second half of summer. It is perfectly happy in moderately fertile or even poor soil, as long as it has good drainage, and requires pruning after flowering only if you need to restrain it and prevent it getting totally out of hand. You can either train this climber up an old, stout tree or allow it to form a huge mound over a tree stump. Impressive, but not the tidiest of plants, it is best grown in a wild or informal garden, well away from anything that might be overwhelmed.

PLANT PROFILE

HEIGHT 12m (40ft)

SITE Full sun or partial shade

SOIL Average, free-draining

HARDINESS Fully hardy

FLOWERING Late summer and autumn

F

Fargesia nitida Bamboo

EXTREMELY TOUGH AND GRACEFUL, this bamboo is slow growing, clump forming and non-invasive. It forms a tall, dense thicket and is therefore best grown as a perimeter hedge in a wild or woodland garden, or as a feature within a very large lawn. The evergreen leaves are dark green, but they do not appear until the second year, leaving the beautiful purple-green canes exposed, creating a stunning effect. There are several good forms of *Fargesia nitida*, including the small-leaved 'Eisenach' and elegant 'Nymphenburg'.

OTHER VARIETIES *F. murielae* (powdery-white canes turn yellow-green, then all-green); *F. murielae* 'Jumbo' (smaller-growing, larger leaves); *F. murielae* 'Simba' (compact, good for small gardens).

PLANT PROFILE

HEIGHT To 5m (15ft)

SPREAD 1.5m (5ft) or more

SITE Partial or light shade

SOIL Moist, fertile

HARDINESS Fully hardy

x *Fatshedera lizei* Tree-ivy

F

SPLENDID, JUNGLY AND SPRAWLING, this cross between an ivy and a fatsia makes a climbing evergreen shrub with shiny leaves up to 25cm (10in) long. The greenish-white flowers appear late in the season and are quite insignificant. Good for livening up an unused, slightly shady corner, it is quite unfussy and thrives in a wide range of conditions, although shelter is a must to prevent the leaves being ruined by cold winds. Pruning is unnecessary except when growth creates an unbalanced shape. 'Variegata' is even more striking.

OTHER VARIETY x *F. lizei* 'Variegata' (leaves with narrow, creamy-white margins).

PLANT PROFILE

HEIGHT 1.2–2m (4–6ft) or more

SPREAD 3m (10ft)

SITE Full sun or partial shade

SOIL Fertile, moist but free-draining

HARDINESS Frost hardy

FLOWERING Autumn

F

Fatsia japonica Japanese aralia

DRAMATIC AND ARCHITECTURAL, this evergreen adds a sculptural element to any garden. Also known as the fig-leafed palm and the false caster oil plant, it will even add shape to a shady corner with its mass of jungle-like, deeply cut, shiny leaves, each about 30cm (12in) wide. It has a spreading habit which means it can be easily underplanted with shade-loving plants, including ferns, hostas and snowdrops. If the aralia becomes too tall and multi-branched (when, incidentally, the leaves become smaller and less dramatic), cut back the main stem quite ruthlessly and new stems will soon regrow. In other circumstances, pruning is unnecessary.

PLANT PROFILE

HEIGHT 1.5–4m (5–12ft)

SPREAD 1.5–4m (5–12ft)

SITE Full sun or light dappled shade

SOIL Moist, fertile, free-draining

HARDINESS Fully hardy

FLOWERING Autumn

Forsythia x *intermedia* 'Lynwood'

F

PROVIDING A COLOURFUL NOTE in spring, when the bare, upright stems of forsythias are smothered in rich yellow flowers. 'Lynwood' makes a fine hedge when used alone or with evergreens. You can also snip off the top of the flowering stems for cut flower displays, or strip the leaves from longer stems in summer and use them to support floppy perennials. It grows in any soil (ideally well-drained), and the more sun it gets the better the flowering. Prune after it has flowered and cut down old stems of mature plants to the ground.

OTHER VARIETIES *F.* 'Beatrix Farrand' (taller-growing, pale yellow flowers); *F.* 'Golden Nugget' (golden-yellow flowers); *F. suspensa* (clusters of yellow flowers, mid- to dark green leaves).

PLANT PROFILE	
HEIGHT 3m (10ft)	
SPREAD 3m (10ft)	
SITE Full sun	
SOIL Free-draining	
HARDINESS Fully hardy	
FLOWERING Early and mid-spring	

F

Fothergilla major

MASSES OF SWEETLY SCENTED white or pink-tinged flowers at the start of the growing season, and fabulous autumn colour, when the shiny dark green leaves turn red, orange and yellow, are the chief assets of this slow-growing, deciduous, North American shrub. The flowers, interestingly, do not have any petals, only bristling stamens. Make sure that the shrub is planted in full sun if you want the best autumn colour and abundant flowers. The soil needs to be acid, with plenty of well-rotted compost added to the planting hole.

OTHER VARIETIES *F. gardenii* (smaller-growing, white flowers, bright red, orange and yellow autumn leaf colour); *F. gardenii* 'Blue Mist' (blue-green leaves).

PLANT PROFILE

HEIGHT 2.5m (8ft)

SPREAD 2m (6ft)

SITE Full sun or partial shade

SOIL Acid, moist but free-draining

HARDINESS Fully hardy

FLOWERING Late spring and early summer

Fremontodendron 'California Glory'

F

OBTAINING A BIG, SHOWY DISPLAY of bright yellow flowers – each about 5cm (2in) wide – from this evergreen North American shrub depends on two factors. First, it needs a warm, sunny, protective wall in all but the mildest gardens and, second, you must provide it with relatively poor to moderately fertile soil with good drainage. Once it is established and growing, it needs to be trained along horizontal wires. It grows at a rate of about 30cm (12in) a year until it reaches its ultimate height, when it makes an impressive sight.

OTHER VARIETIES *F. californicum* (saucer-shaped, yellow flowers, dark green leaves); *F.* 'Pacific Sunset' (bright yellow flowers in summer with long, slender-pointed lobes).

PLANT PROFILE

HEIGHT 6m (20ft)

SPREAD 4m (12ft)

SITE Full sun

SOIL Average, free-draining

HARDINESS Frost hardy

FLOWERING Late spring to mid-autumn

F

Fuchsia 'Genii'

THIS VERSATILE SHRUB can be grown as part of a flowering hedge, as a border plant, in an ornamental container (to be brought indoors in winter) or as a standard. 'Genii' is erect, deciduous and bushy, and is in flower nearly all summer. It needs shelter and protection in cold-climate gardens, plus a thick winter mulch of compost, and plants should be cut back in the spring to encourage new, bushy growth. Grow it in free-draining, rich soil, and water young plants well in their first year as they are getting established.

OTHER VARIETIES *F.* 'Brookwood Belle' (cerise and white double flowers); *F.* 'Display' (carmine and pink single flowers); *F.* 'Riccartonii' (small scarlet and purple flowers).

PLANT PROFILE

HEIGHT 90cm (36in)

SPREAD 90cm (36in)

SITE Full sun

SOIL Fertile, free-draining

HARDINESS Frost hardy

FLOWERING Summer

Garrya elliptica Silk-tassel bush

G

TOUGH AND INDESTRUCTIBLE, this evergreen shrub looks best from midwinter to early spring when it is covered by long, dangling, grey-green catkins. The shrub also makes an excellent, dense, bushy hedge, and can be easily kept in shape with a trim once the display of catkins is over. Given free-draining soil, *Garrya elliptica* also grows well in coastal gardens, but do not use it as a windbreak because it likes a sheltered position. Double check that you are buying male plants because these provide showier catkins than the females.

OTHER VARIETIES *G. elliptica* 'James Roof' (male, longer catkins); *G.* x *issaquahensis* 'Pat Ballard' (smaller-growing, purple-tinged catkins).

PLANT PROFILE
HEIGHT 4m (12ft)
SPREAD 4m (12ft)
SITE Full sun or partial shade
SOIL Free-draining
HARDINESS Frost hardy
FLOWERING Midwinter to early spring

G | *Gaultheria mucronata* 'Mulberry Wine'

THIS COMPACT, VIGOROUS EVERGREEN (formerly known as *Pernettya mucronata*) is popular for its reddish young stems and glossy foliage. The white, late spring flowers might be minuscule but they appear in numbers large enough to give a good display. These are followed by its chief asset (if you have an adjacent male and female) – masses of magenta fruit, ripening to dark purple. It grows best in partial shade, and needs moist soil that is peaty and acid.

OTHER VARIETIES   *G. cuneata* (smaller-growing, white flowers followed by white fruit); *G. mucronata* 'Cherry Ripe' (bright cerise fruit); *G. mucronata* 'Snow White' (white fruit slightly spotted with pink); *G. shallon* (pink-tinged white flowers, purple fruit).

PLANT PROFILE	
HEIGHT 1.2m (4ft)	
SPREAD 1.2m (4ft)	
SITE Partial shade	
SOIL Acid, moist	
HARDINESS Fully hardy	
FLOWERING Late spring	

Gaultheria procumbens Checkerberry

G

WITH ITS LOW, SPREADING GROWTH, the checkerberry makes ideal ground cover. It is vigorous, however, and shouldn't be grown too close to neighbouring plants. The glossy, dark green leaves, release a sweet, gentle scent when torn, and its summer flowers are up 2.5cm (1in) long. The white or pale pink blooms are then followed by attractive scarlet berries which hang on right through winter. It thrives in peaty, moist, acid soil and a shady site. Don't be tempted to plant it in the sun unless the soil is damp and never dries out.

OTHER VARIETY   *G. mucronata* (taller-growing, white flowers, purple-red to white fruit).

PLANT PROFILE
HEIGHT 15cm (6in)
SPREAD To 1m (3ft) or more
SITE Shade
SOIL Acid, moist
HARDINESS Frost hardy
FLOWERING Summer

G | *Genista lydia* Broom

WHILE MOST BROOMS ARE LARGE, upright shrubs, this low-growing, domed form is a real beauty for rock gardens or raised beds, and is also perfect for the top of a wall where its grey-green arching stems will tumble over the edge. In early summer it becomes smothered in tiny, pea-like, yellow flowers and is so floriferous that you can barely see the blue-green deciduous leaves. Light, free-draining soil is essential; average fertility is fine. No pruning is necessary – if the plant becomes too straggly, simply replace it with a new, young one.

OTHER VARIETIES *G. aetnensis* (tree-like, golden-yellow flowers); *G. pilosa* 'Vancouver Gold' (mound forming, yellow flowers); *G. tinctoria* 'Royal Gold' (more upright, yellow flowers in long panicles).

PLANT PROFILE

HEIGHT 60cm (24in)

SPREAD 1m (3ft)

SITE Full sun

SOIL Light to average, free-draining

HARDINESS Fully hardy

FLOWERING Early summer

Grevillea 'Canberra Gem'

THIS QUICK-GROWING EVERGREEN makes a dense, bushy shrub with curiously curly, waxy pink-red flowers. The first buds start to open in late winter and offer a welcome splash of colour at such a dull time of year – flowering then continues well into summer. A native of Australia, cold-climate gardens aren't ideal which means a sunny, sheltered site is vital, for example, at the foot of a sunny wall, or grow it in a large tub and bring it under cover over winter. Keep the soil quite dry in winter. Prune for shape after flowering but avoid contact with your skin as it can cause allergies.

OTHER VARIETY *G. rosmarinifolia* (pink or cream flowers).

PLANT PROFILE
HEIGHT 2–4m (6–12ft)
SPREAD 2–5m (6–15ft)
SITE Full sun
SOIL Acid to neutral, free-draining
HARDINESS Frost hardy
FLOWERING Late winter to late summer, often at other times

G | *Grindelia chiloensis*

THE ONLY POSSIBLE PROBLEM WITH *Grindelia chiloensis* is that it is
not totally hardy. In cold winters this sprawling, evergreen shrub
will behave more like a perennial with the top-growth dying back.
If this happens don't worry because new shoots will appear the
following spring. It produces greyish-green, 12cm (5in) long leaves,
and bears attractive, sunny-yellow daisy-like blooms on long stalks
right through the summer period. This colourful show often extends
well into autumn. For the best results, grow it in the sunniest spot
in the garden – a hot, dry bank would be perfect – and plant in
free-draining, average soil.

PLANT PROFILE

HEIGHT 1m (3ft)

SPREAD 1m (3ft)

SITE Full sun

SOIL Poor to average,
free-draining

HARDINESS Borderline
fully hardy

FLOWERING Summer

Griselinia littoralis 'Variegata' Broadleaf

G

AN EXCELLENT CHOICE for seaside gardens, this plant not only withstands salty winds but, being borderline hardy, benefits from the mild coastal conditions. With its dense, evergreen, apple-green leaves with creamy-white margins, it is also suitable for gardens that require year-round architectural interest or areas of attractive hedging. The striking foliage makes a contrasting backdrop for the vivid, primary colours of a wide range of perennials. The greenish spring flowers are, by contrast, rather inconspicuous. Plant it in fertile, free-draining soil, and prune for shape after flowering.

OTHER VARIETY *G. littoralis* (taller, sometimes tree-like in mild areas, apple-green leaves).

PLANT PROFILE

HEIGHT 3m (10ft)

SPREAD 2m (6ft)

SITE Full sun

SOIL Light, fertile, free-draining

HARDINESS Borderline fully hardy

FLOWERING Late spring

H | X *Halimiocistus sahucii*

BRIEF ENCOUNTERS OFTEN MAKE a great impression. The charming white flowers of this sun-loving plant from the south of France open in the morning only to fade by sunset, but this is certainly not a problem. From early summer there is always a plentiful supply of buds waiting to open on the low, wiry stems, ensuring a good show. To thrive, this Mediterranean, low-spreading evergreen needs shelter from winter winds and poor to average, sharply drained soil. Raised beds, gravel and rock gardens, or gaps between the paving on a sunny terrace are all perfect sites.

OTHER VARIETY X *H. wintonensis* 'Merrist Wood Cream' (pale yellow flowers with a red inner band, borderline hardy).

PLANT PROFILE

HEIGHT 45cm (18in)

SPREAD 90cm (36in)

SITE Full sun

SOIL Poor to average, sandy, free-draining

HARDINESS Fully hardy

FLOWERING Summer

Halimium 'Susan'

THE RICHLY COLOURED, bright yellow flowers of this low-growing, spreading shrub have a red-purple ring right in the middle. Like all halimiums, it needs all the summer sun it can get, plus average, free-draining, dryish soil with some shelter. Take care when siting this plant because it hates being disturbed once it is established. A good choice for the front of a border or a large rock garden, it also makes an excellent container plant. If plants start to look straggly, give them a light trim for shape in spring.

OTHER VARIETIES *H. lasianthum* (slightly larger, golden-yellow flowers with brown centres); *H. ocymoides* (taller-growing, golden-yellow flowers with black-purple centres, white, downy, grey-green leaves).

PLANT PROFILE
HEIGHT 45cm (18in)
SPREAD 60cm (24in)
SITE Full sun
SOIL Moderately fertile, sandy, free-draining
HARDINESS Frost hardy
FLOWERING Summer

H | *Hamamelis* x *intermedia* 'Pallida' Witch hazel

HIGHLY RATED, this spreading, deciduous winter shrub is barnacled with large, sulphur-yellow flowers. Looking more like short tufts of yellow string than a traditional flower, they carry the sweetest fragrance. 'Pallida' is fairly large – really more of a rounded tree than a shrub – and needs a woodland garden or a site on the boundary of a medium-sized garden. A fairly sheltered spot in slightly acid to neutral, moist but free-draining soil suits it best. Prune for shape only in spring.

OTHER VARIETIES *H.* x *intermedia* 'Arnold Promise' (large yellow flowers); *H.* x *intermedia* 'Diane' (dark red flowers, yellow and red autumn foliage); *H.* x *intermedia* 'Jelena' (coppery-orange flowers).

PLANT PROFILE

HEIGHT 4m (12ft)

SPREAD 4m (12ft)

SITE Full sun or partial shade

SOIL Acid to neutral, fertile, moist but free-draining

HARDINESS Fully hardy

FLOWERING Early and midwinter

Hebe 'Great Orme'

H

PLANT PROFILE

LOOKING EQUALLY GOOD in a border or a large container, this hebe makes a rounded evergreen with shiny leaves. The flowers appear in the second half of summer and continue into autumn; when they first open the flowers are pink but they age to white. Like most hebes, 'Great Orme' is not totally hardy and needs a warm, sheltered spot with protection from cold winds, and average, well-drained soil. Bring pot-grown plants into a frost-free greenhouse over winter. Prune to shape in spring.

OTHER VARIETIES *H. albicans* (smaller-growing, white flowers); *H. cupressoides* 'Boughton Dome' (dwarf, pale green, scale-like leaves); *H.* 'Midsummer Beauty' (taller-growing, lilac-purple flowers).

HEIGHT 1.2m (4ft)

SPREAD 1.2m (4ft)

SITE Sun or partial shade

SOIL Average, moist but free-draining

HARDINESS Frost hardy

FLOWERING Midsummer to mid-autumn

First, completely cut out any frost-damaged stems and then lightly trim the whole plant with shears to stimulate new growth.

H *Hebe pinguifolia* 'Pagei'

MOST PEOPLE THINK OF HEBES AS ROUNDED, but 'Pagei' is a prostrate shrub that makes excellent ground cover. Grow it in borders, as an edging for paths and in rock gardens. The bright white flowers are offset by small, round, blue-green leaves. Free-draining soil and shelter from cold winds are essential, and if you wish to prune your hebe to make it more shapely, do it in early spring. As well as crisp white, hebes come in a vast range of colours, including blues, pinks, purples, and reds.

OTHER VARIETIES *H. albicans* (compact mound, white flowers); *H. hulkeana* (taller-growing, lavender-blue, lilac, or white flowers).

PLANT PROFILE

HEIGHT 30cm (12in)

SPREAD 90cm (36in)

SITE Sun or partial shade

SOIL Average, free-draining

HARDINESS Fully hardy

FLOWERING Late spring and early summer

Hedera colchica 'Sulphur Heart' Ivy

H

ONE OF THE BEST VARIEGATED IVIES, 'Sulphur Heart' is a bold, dramatic evergreen climber. The light green leaves, up to 15cm (6in) long, make a colourful splash with their creamy-yellow markings. A rampant spreader, it will quickly cover ugly sheds, walls and fences, but if you are thinking of training it on a house wall, make sure that the surface is in very good condition as its self-clinging suckers could cause damage. Cut it back in spring if it spreads beyond its allotted space and into gutters, window frames or under roof tiles. Avoid planting in heavy, wet soil.

OTHER VARIETIES *H. colchica* 'Dentata' (purple-flushed stems); *H. colchica* 'Dentata Variegata' (white-margined, mottled grey-green leaves).

PLANT PROFILE

HEIGHT 5m (15ft)

SITE Sun

SOIL Fertile, free-draining

HARDINESS Fully hardy

FLOWERING Autumn

H | *Hedera helix* 'Glacier' Common ivy

A VIGOROUS IVY, SUCH AS 'GLACIER', will quickly cloak a small shed or ugly wall with its attractive variegated leaves. Without training, the plant naturally forms a ground-hugging mound, so you need to entice the self-clinging stems to grow upwards for the first few years. You can also train it as a standard by growing it up a sturdy post topped with a ball-shaped wire frame. Note that variegated ivies must be grown in full sun or they will lose their markings. Plant in average soil.

OTHER VARIETIES *H. helix* 'Buttercup' (yellow leaves in full sun, pale green leaves in shade); *H. helix* 'Cavendishii' (creamy-yellow leaf margins); *H. helix* 'Pedata' (leaves are shaped like a bird's foot).

PLANT PROFILE	
HEIGHT 2m (6ft) or more	
SITE Sun	
SOIL Average	
HARDINESS Fully hardy	
FLOWERING Autumn	

Helianthemum 'Raspberry Ripple' Rock rose

H

IDEAL AS GROUND COVER for rock or gravel gardens, this small evergreen stands out with its white flowers, each with a yellow eye and purple-pink markings radiating from the centre. Like other rock roses, it's not too fussy and grows in average, free-draining soil, although a sunny situation is essential for it to thrive. After flowering, cut back flowered shoots to within 2.5cm (1in) of the previous year's growth. Rock roses are available in a wide range of colours.

OTHER VARIETIES *H.* 'Chocolate Blotch' (buff-coloured flowers with chocolate-brown markings); *H.* 'Fire Dragon' (vivid orange-red flowers); *H.* 'The Bride' (white flowers); *H.* 'Wisley Primrose' (pale primrose-yellow flowers).

PLANT PROFILE
HEIGHT 20cm (8in)
SPREAD 30cm (12in)
SITE Full sun
SOIL Average, free-draining
HARDINESS Fully hardy
FLOWERING Late spring to midsummer

H

Helichrysum italicum subsp. *serotinum* Curry plant

CRUSH THE AROMATIC LEAVES of the curry plant and you'll discover why it is so named. It is often planted as a mini-hedge in the border or herb garden where its silver-grey, evergreen foliage is a restful colour break between other plants. It makes a wonderfully bushy shrub, and is studded with dark yellow flowers throughout summer. For the curry plant to thrive you must plant it in quick-draining soil in a sheltered spot – cold, drying winds and excessive winter wet will be fatal. To maintain shape, in spring cut back flowered shoots to within 2.5cm (1in) of the previous year's growth.

OTHER VARIETIES   *H. italicum* (larger, dark yellow flowers); *H. petiolare* (woolly grey leaves); *H. splendidum* (larger, white stems, yellow flowers).

PLANT PROFILE
HEIGHT 40cm (16in)
SPREAD 75cm (30in)
SITE Full sun
SOIL Average, free-draining
HARDINESS Frost hardy
FLOWERING Summer to autumn

Hibiscus syriacus 'Oiseau Bleu'

H

HIBISCUS ARE COLOURFUL PLANTS with flowers in shades of white through to deep purple, but the bright blue of 'Oiseau Bleu' takes some beating. Try growing two contrastingly coloured plants together, allowing their flowers to intermingle. *Hibiscus syriacus* is a hardy, deciduous shrub that performs best in rich, moist but well-drained soil. Full sun isn't an option, it's a necessity and the hotter the summer the better flowering will be. Prune when young to encourage bushiness but thereafter pruning is not needed.

OTHER VARIETIES *H. syriacus* 'Diana' (very large white flowers); *H. syriacus* 'Pink Giant' (large red-centred pink flowers); *H. syriacus* 'Red Heart' (red-centred white flowers).

PLANT PROFILE	
HEIGHT 3m (10ft)	
SPREAD 2m (6ft)	
SITE Full sun	
SOIL Fertile, moist but free-draining	
HARDINESS Fully hardy	
FLOWERING Late summer to mid-autumn	

H | *Hippophae rhamnoides* Sea buckthorn

ESSENTIAL IN ANY EXPOSED COASTAL GARDEN, the sea buckthorn happily tolerates gales and thin, sandy soil, creating a highly effective summer windbreak. In winter, however, because it is deciduous it will lose its protecting thicket of grey–green leaves. The advantage of growing a few plants together is that you can mix males among the female plants so that they will produce their bright orange berries. As birds dislike the bitter taste of the fruit, they are left untouched over winter to give the hedge a bit of colour. Pruning is usually unnecessary, but to improve overall shapeliness you can cut out badly congested or wayward stems in late summer.

OTHER VARIETY *H. rhamnoides* 'Leikora' (very profuse berries).

PLANT PROFILE
HEIGHT 6m (20ft)
SPREAD 6m (20ft)
SITE Full sun
SOIL Moist but free-draining, preferably sandy
HARDINESS Fully hardy
FLOWERING Spring

Hoheria glabrata

AN ATTRACTIVE FOCAL POINT in a woodland garden or the centre of a spacious lawn, it's hardly surprising that this impressive, vigorous deciduous shrub is often listed as a tree. In the first half of summer the arching stems are tightly packed with scented, white flowers (*see inset*) that are attractive to butterflies. It is not usually planted away from coastal sites which is a shame because it thrives in sheltered, sunny gardens in any mild region where the soil is free-draining. If the top-growth dies back in winter, new shoots should appear from the base the following spring.

OTHER VARIETY *H. sexstylosa* (evergreen, white flowers).

PLANT PROFILE
HEIGHT 7m (22ft)
SPREAD 7m (22ft)
SITE Sun or partial shade
SOIL Average, free-draining
HARDINESS Frost hardy
FLOWERING Midsummer

H | *Holboellia coriacea*

ONE OF THE BEST, and also one of the most underrated climbers, *Holboellia coriacea* is an evergreen vine with heavenly, fragrant flowers. To help its woody stems climb it needs a strong frame, such as a wall strung with horizontal wires, or a stout tree trunk. The male flowers, which appear on the previous year's growth, are mauve, while the greenish-white females are produced on new current growth. After a hot summer purple fruit may be produced. Provide free-draining, rich soil and a sunny, sheltered site. Pruning is not essential.

OTHER VARIETY *H. latifolia* (shorter-growing, white male and purple female flowers).

PLANT PROFILE

HEIGHT 7m (22ft)

SITE Full sun or partial shade

SOIL Fertile, free-draining

HARDINESS Frost hardy

FLOWERING Spring

Holodiscus discolor Ocean spray

H

THIS GIANT, UPRIGHT, ARCHING SHRUB is usually planted on the perimeter of a garden. In midsummer, its long grey-green leaves are almost hidden by an eruption of creamy-white, cup-shaped flowers which hang in airy, plume-like sprays up to 30cm (12in) long. Pruning is usually unnecessary but, after flowering, you can help to reinvigorate mature plants and encourage them to produce new shoots by cutting out one in four of the old stems to a healthy bud on lower growth. For ocean spray to reach its full potential it must have a rich, moist but free-draining soil in sun or light shade.

PLANT PROFILE

HEIGHT 4m (12ft)

SPREAD 4m (12ft)

SITE Sun or partial shade

SOIL Fertile, moist but free-draining

HARDINESS Fully hardy

FLOWERING Midsummer

H *Humulus lupulus* 'Aureus' Hop

Hops are fast-climbing perennials that shoot up in spring. 'Aureus' produces a bright summery mass of large, yellow-green leaves and looks wonderful grown over a pergola, against a wall or fence, between other climbers or up a tall tree. A good support is essential to stop top growth being damaged in blustery winds. The flowers on female plants mature into 5cm (2in) long hops. Fertile, moist but free-draining soil is best, and for the brightest leaf colour grow it in full sun. As a screen it will only be effective in summer because the plant dies down during the winter.

OTHER VARIETY *H. lupulus* (light green leaves, fragrant, green female flowers become straw-coloured).

PLANT PROFILE
HEIGHT 6m (20ft)
SITE Sun or partial shade
SOIL Fertile, moist but free-draining
HARDINESS Fully hardy
FLOWERING Summer

Hydrangea anomala subsp. *petiolaris* Climbing hydrangea

H

LOOKING NOTHING LIKE the ornamental hydrangeas typically found in borders, this woody-stemmed deciduous climber will quickly cover a huge stretch of wall or climb up into a solid, mature tree clinging on with its strong aerial roots. If you prefer, it is also sturdy enough to be grown as a freestanding shrub or bush. It makes a superb mass of dark green leaves, up to 11cm (4½in) long, which turn yellow in autumn before falling. The creamy-white flowers last only two to three weeks in summer. It performs best in sun but will cope well with cool shade. Prune after flowering if the plant is in danger of outgrowing the available space.

PLANT PROFILE	
HEIGHT 15m (50ft)	
SITE Sun or partial shade	
SOIL Fertile, moist but free-draining	
HARDINESS Fully hardy	
FLOWERING Summer	

H | *Hydrangea macrophylla* 'Ayesha'

A CURIOUSLY BEAUTIFUL HYDRANGEA, 'Ayesha' has flowers like those of a lilac (*Syringa*) and glossy leaves. Soil chemistry affects all the macrophylla types: on acid soil their flowers are lilac, while on other soils they come up pink – only the whites stay white. Shelter from cold, drying winds is important, as is moist but free-draining soil. Annual pruning will improve the show of flowers: cut mature plants back hard in spring to a couple of vigorous buds, removing one-third of each stem. Skin contact can give rise to allergies.

OTHER VARIETIES *H. macrophylla* 'Blue Bonnet' (rich blue to pink flowers); *H. macrophylla* 'Europa' (dark pink to purple-blue flowers); *H. macrophylla* 'White Wave' (white sterile and pink to blue fertile flowers).

PLANT PROFILE

HEIGHT 1.5m (5ft)

SPREAD 2m (6ft)

SITE Sun or partial shade

SOIL Fertile, moist but free-draining

HARDINESS Fully hardy

FLOWERING Mid- and late summer

Hydrangea paniculata 'Grandiflora'

H

THIS ORNAMENTAL DECIDUOUS HYDRANGEA is one of the best, with large flowerheads up to 30cm (12in) tall. They open pure white but soon acquire a pink tinge. Prune in the spring to within a few buds of the woody framework to encourage even larger flowerheads. 'Grandiflora' needs to be grown towards the back of a spacious border where the heavy blooms can droop forward unhampered, particularly after rain. Grow in rich, moist but well-drained soil, and protect it from cold, drying winds.

OTHER VARIETIES *H. paniculata* 'Floribunda' (pink-tinged white sterile flowers); *H. paniculata* 'Kyushu' (glossy leaves); *H. paniculata* 'Praecox' (flowers earlier, from midsummer).

PLANT PROFILE
HEIGHT 3–7m (10–22ft)
SPREAD 2.5m (8ft)
SITE Sun or partial shade
SOIL Fertile, moist but free-draining
HARDINESS Fully hardy
FLOWERING Late summer and early autumn

H

Hydrangea serrata 'Bluebird'

IF YOU WANT A DECIDUOUS HYDRANGEA that is compact, erect and never gets too large, choose 'Bluebird'. It is reliably hardy and will withstand severe spring frosts. The prolific displays of flattish flowerheads will be rich blue on acid soil and reddish-purple on chalky, alkaline ground. The flowers dry particularly well for indoor arrangements. The shrub has a final fling in autumn when its foliage reddens up before falling. For best results grow it in rich, moist but well-drained soil in a spot that's sheltered from cold, drying winds.

OTHER VARIETIES *H. macrophylla* (taller-growing); *H.* 'Preziosa' (small heads of white flowers); *H. quercifolia* (taller-growing, mound-forming, pink-tinged white flowers, green leaves turn bronze-purple).

PLANT PROFILE
HEIGHT 1.2m (4ft)
SPREAD 1.2m (4ft)
SITE Sun or partial shade
SOIL Fertile, moist but free-draining
HARDINESS Frost hardy
FLOWERING Summer to autumn

Hypericum 'Hidcote'

HIGHLY EFFECTIVE AND PERFECTLY RELIABLE, this shrub can be grown in a wide range of gardens given average to fertile, free-draining soil. It is just the right size for most borders and, as well as a prolific show of flowers, provides a dense covering of glossy, evergreen leaves. The butter-yellow, five-petalled blooms appear in the second half of summer. Prune lightly to shape after flowering.

OTHER VARIETIES *H. calycinum* (shorter, wide-spreading); *H. forrestii* (mid-green leaves turning red in late autumn); *H. kouytchense* (flowers followed by red fruit, bluish-green leaves); *H.* 'Rowallane' (taller, golden-yellow flowers late summer to autumn, semi-evergreen).

PLANT PROFILE
HEIGHT 1.2m (4ft)
SPREAD 1.5m (5ft)
SITE Sun or partial shade
SOIL Average, moist but free-draining
HARDINESS Fully hardy
FLOWERING Midsummer to early autumn

H | *Hyssopus officinalis* Hyssop

THE CHIEF VIRTUE of this aromatic, semi-evergreen shrub is its dark blue, mid- to late-season flowers which are a magnet to bees and butterflies. A versatile herb from southern Europe, use the flowers in salads, and its leaves for cooking and in pot-pourris and infusions (avoid in any form if pregnant). It also makes a beautiful border plant when grown as a miniature hedge to divide up a large bed. A sun lover, it must also have light, free-draining soil. In spring, clip it lightly for shape with shears, or cut back hard to renovate.

OTHER VARIETIES *H. officinalis* f. *albus* (white flowers); *H. officinalis* subsp. *aristatus* (dense, upright, bright green leaves); *H. officinalis* 'Roseus' (pink flowers).

PLANT PROFILE	
HEIGHT 60cm (24in)	
SPREAD 1m (3ft)	
SITE Full sun	
SOIL Light, free-draining	
HARDINESS Fully hardy	
FLOWERING Midsummer to early autumn	

Ilex aquifolium 'Handsworth New Silver' Common holly

THE SPINY, DARK GREEN LEAVES of this evergreen shrub or tree have attractive creamy margins. Note that 'Handsworth New Silver' is a female holly and will bear cheery bright red berries, following cross pollination from a nearby male. Likely males include the rather confusingly named 'Golden Queen' and 'Silver Queen'. Hollies can be grown as individual specimens, hedges or be topiarized – pruning for shape should be done in early spring. Plant in full sun or light shade for the strongest variegation.

OTHER VARIETIES   *I. aquifolium* 'Argentea Marginata' (female, cream-streaked leaves with white margins, red berries); *I. aquifolium* 'Madame Briot' (female, purple stems, gold-margined leaves, red fruit).

PLANT PROFILE
HEIGHT 8m (25ft)
SPREAD 5m (15ft)
SITE Full sun
SOIL Moist but free-draining
HARDINESS Fully hardy
FLOWERING Spring to early summer

HARD PRUNING

In warm areas very little pruning is required, but in cold gardens the stems can be damaged by frost and are best cut to near ground level in spring.

I

Indigofera heterantha

GREAT VALUE FOR MONEY, this deciduous shrub manages to pull something out of the hat to sustain interest nearly all year round. It's a winning mix of arching branches with fern-like leaves and pretty, pea-like, purple-pink flowers which appear over a long season. Although it is fully hardy it prefers a sunny, sheltered site – after a freezing winter don't be alarmed to see it cut down by frost as it will reshoot. If you want to restrict its size, cut stems back down to the ground each spring to force up new flowering shoots. In a romantic or cottage garden setting *Indigofera heterantha* will be a star.

OTHER VARIETIES *I. amblyantha* (pink flowers); *I. kirilowii* (smaller-growing, rose-pink flowers).

PLANT PROFILE

HEIGHT 2–3m (6–10ft)

SPREAD 2–3m (6–10ft)

SITE Full sun

SOIL Moist but free-draining

HARDINESS Fully hardy

FLOWERING Early summer to early autumn

Ipomoea indica Blue dawn flower

WINTER WARMTH IS NEEDED to keep this climber growing all year; if you're going to plant it outdoors, treat it as an annual and discard it at the end of summer. A vigorous twiner, grow it up horizontal wires against a conservatory wall, or over a wigwam of canes or a pergola in the garden. The flowers are a sumptuous rich blue with a hint of regal purple, but individual blooms don't last long, opening in the morning and dying by the end of the day. In season, however, new buds are always waiting to open in rapid succession.

OTHER VARIETIES *I. nil* 'Scarlett O'Hara' (bright red flowers); *I. tricolor* 'Crimson Rambler' (smaller-growing, red flowers with white throats); *I. tricolor* 'Heavenly Blue' (azure flowers with white throats).

PLANT PROFILE

HEIGHT 6m (20ft) or more

SITE Full sun

SOIL Fertile, free-draining

HARDINESS Frost tender

FLOWERING Late spring to autumn

I

Itea ilicifolia

THERE'S SOMETHING IRRESISTIBLE about honey-scented flowers, and the thin, dangling catkins of *Itea ilicifolia*, which reach up to 30cm (12in) long, are particularly sweet. Grow this evergreen shrub as a feature plant or hedge, or train it against a wall as a living climbing frame for clematis. Plant it somewhere sheltered because cold winter winds will damage the holly-like foliage. Grow in reasonably fertile, moist soil – young plants will need watering during dry spells as their roots take a while to become established. In spring, a thick mulch of compost after watering or heavy rain will help seal in moisture.

OTHER VARIETY *I. virginica* (shorter-growing, fragrant, white flowers, prefers slightly acid soil in partial shade).

PLANT PROFILE

HEIGHT 3–5m (10–15ft)

SPREAD 3m (10ft)

SITE Full sun

SOIL Fertile, moist but free-draining

HARDINESS Frost hardy

FLOWERING Midsummer to early autumn

Jasminum nudiflorum Winter jasmine

J

THE UNDISPUTED STAR OF THE WINTER GARDEN, *Jasminum nudiflorum* produces a flash of bright yellow on bare stems long before there is any hint of spring in the air. The deciduous leaves won't appear until the flowers fade. The thin, arching stems are easily trained against a wall or fence to create a fan of flowers and you can jazz up the effect by planting it beside a red-berrying cotoneaster. Winter jasmine is a remarkably unfussy plant and will tolerate most garden sites, but given a choice it would prefer sun or light shade (where it will flower slightly better) in fertile, well-drained soil. Prune after flowering by cutting back the flowered stems to a healthy new bud. This is also the time to renovate congested plants by reducing the bush by a quarter.

PLANT PROFILE
HEIGHT 3m (10ft)
SPREAD 3m (10ft)
SITE Full sun or light shade
SOIL Fertile, free-draining
HARDINESS Fully hardy
FLOWERING Winter and early spring

J

Jasminum officinale Common jasmine

THE TWINING STEMS of this fabulously scented deciduous or semi-evergreen climber can be grown over a pergola, trellis or arch. It needs a sheltered, sunny position for three reasons: first, it is not totally hardy; second, while it tolerates shade it flowers best in full sun; and third, the scent from its white flowers will linger in an enclosed space. When planting, allow plenty of room for its rampant growth. Prune only to remove frost-damaged growth or, after flowering, to thin out congested stems.

OTHER VARIETIES *J. beesianum* (shorter-growing, pinkish-red flowers); *J. officinale* 'Argenteovariegatum' (white-margined, grey-green leaves); *J. officinale* 'Aureovariegatum' (leaves marked with yellow).

PLANT PROFILE
HEIGHT 12m (40ft)
SITE Full sun
SOIL Light, free-draining
HARDINESS Frost hardy
FLOWERING Summer to early autumn

Kalmia latifolia Calico bush

K

A DENSELY GROWING EVERGREEN, the calico bush is awash in pink (sometimes white) flowers in the first half of summer. Grow this beautiful shrub as a hedge or as an individual specimen plant on acid soils. It is also suitable for planting on the fringes of a woodland garden. In the second half of summer, after flowering is over, the glossy, dark green leaves make a good backdrop for late-summer shrubs. Pander to its preference for moist, rich soil by adding a really thick mulch of garden compost over the root area in spring.

OTHER VARIETIES *K. latifolia* 'Freckles' (pink flowers with dark spots); *K. latifolia* 'Shooting Star' (white flowers); *K. latifolia* 'Silver Dollar' (white flowers).

PLANT PROFILE

HEIGHT 3m (10ft)

SPREAD 3m (10ft)

SITE Sun or partial shade

SOIL Acid, moist, fertile

HARDINESS Fully hardy

FLOWERING Late spring to midsummer

K *Kerria japonica* 'Pleniflora' Jew's mantle

WHEN PLANTING KERRIA, make allowances for its vigorous, suckering habit. 'Pleniflora' will spread to 3m (10ft) in time, producing masses of vertical, thin, twiggy stems that bear long-lasting, pompon-like double flowers. Its generous proportions mean that it is best grown as part of a perimeter hedge, in a large border or in a woodland garden. After flowering, the bright green leaves are the main feature until they fall in autumn. All kerria needs is free-draining soil in sun or light shade. Cutting flowered stems back to different levels will produce blooms at different heights the following year.

OTHER VARIETIES *K. japonica* 'Golden Guinea' (single yellow flowers); *K. japonica* 'Picta' (smaller, creamy-margined grey-green leaves).

PLANT PROFILE
HEIGHT 3m (10ft)
SPREAD 3m (10ft)
SITE Full sun or partial shade
SOIL Fertile, free-draining
HARDINESS Fully hardy
FLOWERING Mid- and late spring

Kolkwitzia amabilis 'Pink Cloud' Beauty bush

K

THE COMMON NAME OF THIS PLANT is completely justified because every arching stem on this dense, deciduous, twiggy shrub becomes laden with deep pink flowers, each with a yellow throat. It is a remarkable sight at the end of spring, before the summer garden gets into full swing. Start as you mean to go on and give it a large space to grow into – it would be criminal to have to cut it back to keep it within bounds. Fertile, well-drained soil and plenty of summer sun are all the goodies it requires. Thin out the stems after flowering by cutting back to a strong bud, to help maintain vigour.

OTHER VARIETY *K. amabilis* (lighter pink flowers).

PLANT PROFILE
HEIGHT 3m (10ft)
SPREAD 4m (12ft)
SITE Full sun
SOIL Fertile, free-draining
HARDINESS Fully hardy
FLOWERING Late spring and early summer

L

Lapageria rosea Chilean bellflower

THE NATIONAL FLOWER OF CHILE, *Lapageria rosea* is a well-behaved evergreen climber that thrives on slightly acid soils. It is an impressive plant with long-lasting, bell-shaped, waxy flowers that appear from midsummer onwards. The twining stems of dark green leaves need a slightly shady wall with horizontal wires to hang on to, or a pergola to climb over. In cold areas it will need the shelter of a warm wall and protection from wind. Pruning should be kept to a minimum, but it's fine to remove crowded or damaged growth after flowering.

OTHER VARIETIES *L. rosea* var. *albiflora* (white flowers); *L. rosea* 'Nash Court' (soft pink flowers with darker pink mottling).

PLANT PROFILE

HEIGHT 5m (15ft)

SITE Partial shade

SOIL Slightly acid, fertile, moist but free-draining

HARDINESS Borderline frost hardy

FLOWERING Midsummer to late autumn

Lathyrus latifolius Everlasting pea

L

NOT TO BE CONFUSED with the highly scented *Lathyrus odoratus* (sweet pea), the everlasting pea is a cottage-garden beauty that produces prolific clusters of rich pink flowers. Cut the top-growth back to ground level in spring to encourage new shoots, and train it to grow up a wigwam of bamboo canes – wrap the structure in wire so that the tendrils have something to cling to. It can also be grown next to and encouraged to spread over shrubs, or teamed with the white flowers of 'White Pearl' for an eye-catching display. Water well in dry spells, and keep pinching out the growing tips to encourage bushiness. Regular deadheading will boost flowering.

OTHER VARIETY *L. vernus* (smaller-growing, purplish-blue flowers).

PLANT PROFILE

HEIGHT 2m (6ft) or more

SPREAD 1m (3ft)

SITE Full sun or light shade

SOIL Fertile, free-draining

HARDINESS Fully hardy

FLOWERING Summer to early autumn

L

Laurus nobilis Bay laurel

MORE FAMILIARLY KNOWN AS THE BAY TREE, this laurel rarely becomes a tree outside the Mediterranean. In colder, wetter regions it is typically sold as a stylish standard, with a bare trunk about 1.2m (4ft) high, topped by a ball of evergreen aromatic leaves, which can be snipped for use in the kitchen. In spring, small greenish-yellow flowers appear, followed on female plants by black berries. Plants grown in the border need to be sheltered from cold, drying winds that will damage the foliage, while pot-grown plants should be brought under cover in winter. In mild, inner-city gardens, and by the sea, it can be grown as a neat hedge. Clip to shape in summer.

OTHER VARIETY *L. nobilis* 'Aurea' (golden-yellow leaves).

PLANT PROFILE
HEIGHT 12m (40ft)
SPREAD 10m (30ft)
SITE Full sun or partial shade
SOIL Fertile, moist but free-draining
HARDINESS Frost hardy
FLOWERING Spring

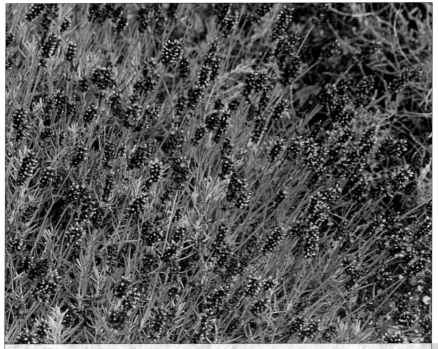

Lavandula angustifolia 'Hidcote' Lavender

L

MORE THAN JUST A SCENTED SHRUB, lavender adds shape and form to the garden. It is also a valuable food source for bees and many butterflies. Dark purple-flowering 'Hidcote' is neatly compact and makes a lovely edging plant for the front of a border or along a path. When cut and dried, the pungent oils in the flowers make a fragrant base for pot-pourri. To grow well, free-draining soil and full sun are essential. Clip it in spring, but don't cut into the old wood.

OTHER VARIETIES *L. angustifolia* 'Munstead' (shorter, blue-purple flowers); *L. angustifolia* 'Nana Alba' (shorter, white flowers); *L. angustifolia* 'Twickel Purple' (purple flowers).

PLANT PROFILE

HEIGHT 60cm (24in)

SPREAD 75cm (30in)

SITE Full sun

SOIL Free-draining

HARDINESS Fully hardy

FLOWERING Mid- and late summer

Cut out all weak growth in spring and prune the remaining stems to 30cm (12in) from the ground. In windy, exposed gardens, prevent winter damage by shortening stems by half their length in autumn.

Lavatera 'Barnsley'

A QUICK-GROWING SEMI-EVERGREEN, 'Barnsley' thickens up in early summer with dozens of arching stems and then produces masses of delicate red-eyed white flowers. Get it off to a good start with very free-draining soil and plenty of sun. It will also welcome the support and shelter of a sunny wall or fence. Lavateras are not long lived and after six or so years need replacing; alternatively take cuttings in early summer to provide new plants. In winter, brush off heavy snow before it snaps the branches, and in spring, cut back frost-damaged stems.

OTHER VARIETIES *L. assurgentiflora* (cerise flowers); *L.* 'Bredon Springs' (mauvish flowers); *L.* 'Burgundy Wine' (dark-veined pink flowers).

PLANT PROFILE	
HEIGHT 2m (6ft)	
SPREAD 2m (6ft)	
SITE Full sun	
SOIL Light to average, free-draining	
HARDINESS Fully hardy	
FLOWERING Summer	

Ledum groenlandicum Labrador tea

L

PLANT PROFILE

IF YOU ARE LOOKING FOR A USEFUL, upright, evergreen shrub for the border or heather garden, then consider Labrador tea. There's no need to worry about its hardiness as it is a native of some pretty chilly places – Greenland, Alaska and Canada – and is named after the Canadian Atlantic coastal region. It produces sprays of white flowers from late spring, and needs rich, moist but well-drained soil that is acid to neutral. Pruning is not usually necessary but an all-over trim after flowering will keep it looking neat.

OTHER VARIETY   *L. palustre* (variable height, white spring flowers).

PLANT PROFILE
HEIGHT 1m (3ft)
SPREAD 1.2m (4ft)
SITE Full sun or partial shade
SOIL Preferably acid, moist, fertile, free-draining
HARDINESS Fully hardy
FLOWERING Late spring

L | *Leonotis leonurus* Lion's ear

FEATURING STRONG SHADES OF RED AND ORANGE, lion's ear is a good choice for a late-season, brightly coloured border. Deciduous or semi-evergreen, this South African shrub features an attractive mix of foliage and flowers. The leaves are thin and needle-like, up to about 12cm (5in) long, and the flower clusters appear in tiers up the tall stems from autumn through to winter. A very tender plant, it needs a mild, sheltered, sunny garden site with free-draining soil to survive over winter. Play safe and pot it up in late autumn to bring into the warmth of a conservatory for the winter. Once flowering is over, prune lightly in spring to maintain shape, if necessary.

PLANT PROFILE

HEIGHT 2m (6ft)

SPREAD 1m (3ft)

SITE Full sun

SOIL Free-draining

HARDINESS Half hardy

FLOWERING Autumn to early winter

Leptospermum scoparium 'Red Damask' New Zealand tea tree

L

ALTHOUGH CALLED A TREE, 'Red Damask' is actually a medium-sized evergreen shrub. It has small, aromatic leaves and, at the start of summer, is covered in small, dark red flowers. Give it the lightest, all-over trim after flowering to increase bushiness and flowering. It requires free-draining, moderately fertile soil and a sunny, sheltered, frost-free site is essential as it is not hardy. If 'Red Damask' grows successfully in your garden, try some of the other attractive forms, especially the frost-hardy, 5m (16ft) tall *Leptospermum lanigerum*.

OTHER VARIETIES *L. scoparium* 'Nichollsii' (crimson flowers, purple-tinged leaves); *L. scoparium* 'Snow Flurry' (double white flowers).

PLANT PROFILE
HEIGHT 3m (10ft)
SPREAD 3m (10ft)
SITE Full sun or partial shade
SOIL Average, free-draining
HARDINESS Half hardy
FLOWERING Late spring and early summer

L   *Lespedeza thunbergii* Bush clover

AMONG THE VERY BEST of the hardy flowering autumn shrubs, it's surprising that *Lespedeza thunbergii* isn't more widely grown. It is slow to get going, not developing leaves until the early summer, but the arching, spreading stems produce a pleasant, relaxed feel. The autumn show consists of airy sprays of small, striking, purple-pink flowers. It tends to be cut back in cold winters but reliably puts out new growth the following spring. Because it develops later than other plants, you may think it has died, but don't give up on it too quickly. Ideally, bush clover likes average, free-draining soil but it should also survive on heavier clay.

OTHER VARIETY *L. bicolor* (purple-pink flowers, dark green leaves).

PLANT PROFILE	
HEIGHT 2m (6ft)	
SPREAD 3m (10ft)	
SITE Full sun	
SOIL Average, light, free-draining	
HARDINESS Fully hardy	
FLOWERING Early autumn	

Leucothoe fontanesiana 'Rainbow'

L

FOR GOOD GROUND COVER ON ACID SOIL, you can't do much better than this eye-catching evergreen shrub. It is upright with arching stems and leathery cream, green and pink mottled leaves that redden up in autumn. In late spring, tiny white flowers appear in dangling clusters. A shady wooded area of the garden, with its rich, reliably moist soil, is an ideal spot. In early spring, cut away any crossing or badly placed stems to improve the overall shape.

OTHER VARIETIES *L. fontanesiana* (larger-growing, white flowers); *L. fontanesiana* 'Rollissonii' (narrow lance-shaped leaves); *L.* 'Zeblid' (red-purple young leaves, turning bronze in autumn).

PLANT PROFILE	
HEIGHT 1.5m (5ft)	
SPREAD 2m (6ft)	
SITE Deep or partial shade	
SOIL Acid, moist, fertile	
HARDINESS Fully hardy	
FLOWERING Late spring	

In spring, cut out spindly, congested growth and then prune some stems – especially old and weak ones – back to soil level.

L *Leycesteria formosa* Himalayan honeysuckle

IN SUMMER, THE HIMALAYAN HONEYSUCKLE is a solid thicket of bamboo-like leafy growth, and dangling flower stems of unusual richly coloured bracts that hold the small white blooms. The flowers are then followed by dark purple berries that last well into autumn. In winter, although it is deciduous, its green stems are striking enough to maintain interest. A free-draining, moderately fertile soil and a sheltered position out of the wind suits it best. Be warned that unless you weed thoroughly around the base of the plant, you will end up with dozens of quick-rooting seedlings. Each spring, prune several stems to the ground to force up fresh, new, leafy growth.

OTHER VARIETY *L. crocothyrsos* (golden-yellow flowers, green berries).

PLANT PROFILE
HEIGHT 2m (6ft)
SPREAD 2m (6ft)
SITE Full sun or partial shade
SOIL Average, free-draining
HARDINESS Fully hardy
FLOWERING Summer to early autumn

Ligustrum ovalifolium 'Aureum' Golden privet

L

DON'T DISMISS PRIVETS AS BEING DULL – many make first-rate shrubs, with strong, dense, evergreen foliage and strongly scented flowers that are followed by tiny, glossy, black berries. 'Aureum' has broad yellow leaf markings ('Argenteum' is similar with white markings) and can be grown in all types of soil, from rich to poor. Note that when grown in poor soil on an exposed site it can become semi-evergreen. Prune in early spring to remove poorly placed stems. If you wish to treat it as a low-growing hedge, it will withstand severe pruning in early and late summer. For the best leaf colour, grow in full sun.

OTHER VARIETIES *L. obtusifolium* (dark green leaves later purple-tinged); *L. quihoui* (taller, mid-green leaves); *L.* 'Vicaryi' (yellow leaves).

PLANT PROFILE
HEIGHT 4m (12ft)
SPREAD 4m (12ft)
SITE Full sun or partial shade
SOIL Average, free-draining
HARDINESS Fully hardy
FLOWERING Midsummer

Lindera obtusiloba

IDEALLY SUITED TO A WOODLAND GARDEN, *Lindera obtusiloba* makes a large shrub or a small tree. For the best results it must have moist but free-draining, acid soil and light shade. Provided these conditions are met, you will be rewarded with a magnificent deciduous shrub with aromatic, glossy, dark green leaves that turn mustard-yellow in autumn. Dark yellow, star-shaped flowers appear in early spring and are followed on female plants – if there is a male plant nearby for pollination – by glossy red-brown berries.

OTHER VARIETY *L. benzoin* (smaller-growing, aromatic bright green leaves, yellow in autumn, greenish-yellow flowers followed by red berries on female plants).

PLANT PROFILE
HEIGHT 6m (20ft)
SPREAD 6m (20ft)
SITE Partial shade
SOIL Acid, fertile, moist but free-draining
HARDINESS Fully hardy
FLOWERING Early and mid-spring

Lithodora diffusa 'Heavenly Blue'

L

LOW-GROWING PLANTS need careful positioning, and one as beautiful as 'Heavenly Blue' should go right at the front of a border, beside a path, or in a rock garden or raised bed where it can be seen clearly. Rarely growing more than ankle high, its energies are put into spreading sideways, and from the end of spring it becomes a carpet of azure-blue flowers. It is a lover of acid soil – which is easy enough to provide in a self-contained raised bed – and good drainage, boosted by digging in plenty of horticultural grit. For an effective contrast, grow blue- and white-flowering types together.

OTHER VARIETIES *L. diffusa* 'Alba' (white flowers); *L. rosmarinifolia* (taller, gentian-blue flowers); *L. zahnii* (taller, blue or white flowers).

PLANT PROFILE

HEIGHT 15cm (6in)

SPREAD 60cm (24in)

SITE Full sun

SOIL Acid, fertile, free-draining

HARDINESS Fully hardy

FLOWERING Late spring and summer

L | *Lomatia ferruginea*

FOR SITES WITH POOR, ACID SOIL, there are precious few evergreen, architectural, bushy shrubs or small trees from which to choose, but this is one of the best. The spindly, fern-like leaves with their fawn underfelting will add a touch of exotica to the garden and, in midsummer, the branches are hung with large swags of yellow and red star-shaped flowers. Being frost hardy it needs shelter from the worst of the winter weather, especially cold, drying winds, and is best sited beside a warm sunny wall or in a wooded area of the garden or shrub border, where it is surrounded by other plants.

OTHER VARIETY *L. tinctoria* (shorter-growing, fragrant, creamy-white flowers).

PLANT PROFILE
HEIGHT 10m (30ft)
SPREAD 5m (15ft)
SITE Full sun or partial shade
SOIL Acid, moist but free-draining
HARDINESS Frost hardy
FLOWERING Midsummer

Lonicera fragrantissima Honeysuckle

L

FORGET THE SUMMER-FLOWERING CLIMBERS, this is a deciduous or semi-evergreen shrub that blooms from the end of winter into spring, filling the garden with its rich fragrance. Given the lack of winter-scented plants, this one is extremely valuable. For the best show of flowers, grow it against a sunny, sheltered wall in rich, moist but well-drained soil. After flowering, prune back the flowered stems to a strong bud, and encourage vigorous new growth on established plants by cutting one in four of the old stems to the ground.

OTHER VARIETIES *L. involucrata* (dark yellow flowers tinged red); *L. korolkowii* (larger-growing, rose-pink flowers).

PLANT PROFILE
HEIGHT 2m (6ft)
SPREAD 3m (10ft)
SITE Full sun or partial shade
SOIL Fertile, moist but free-draining
HARDINESS Fully hardy
FLOWERING Winter and early spring

L | *Lonicera japonica* 'Halliana' Japanese honeysuckle

THIS FAST-GROWING, QUICK-SPREADING evergreen or semi-evergreen climber guarantees masses of leafy growth and pure white, richly scented flowers. The flowers later turn yellow and are followed by tiny black berries. An extremely vigorous grower, it needs a large expanse of wall or a stout, strong tree, pergola or an old shed to sprawl over. A typical honeysuckle, it prefers rich, moist but well-drained soil with shade at the base of the stem. If it outgrows its allotted space, cut back long stems in early spring to a healthy bud.

OTHER VARIETY *L. japonica* var. *repens* (purple-tinged foliage, white flowers are flushed red-purple).

PLANT PROFILE

HEIGHT 10m (30ft)

SITE Full sun or partial shade

SOIL Fertile, moist but free-draining

HARDINESS Fully hardy

FLOWERING Spring to late summer

Lonicera nitida 'Baggesen's Gold' Honeysuckle

L

THE GREAT ATTRACTION of this dense, bushy evergreen shrub lies in its yellow leaves. Make a feature of them by pruning its mass of stems into shapely topiary, or use it like box (*Buxus*) as a mini hedge for parterres and knot gardens. If left unpruned, white spring flowers are followed by tiny, blue–purple berries. To keep it tidy it needs trimming at least three times a year between spring and autumn. Any free-draining, fertile soil is suitable.

OTHER VARIETIES *L. involucrata* (smaller-growing, red-tinged dark yellow flowers); *L. nitida* (creamy-white flowers, blue-purple berries); *L. x purpusii* 'Winter Beauty' (smaller-growing, white and yellow flowers).

PLANT PROFILE	
HEIGHT 3.5m (11ft)	
SPREAD 3m (10ft)	
SITE Full sun or partial shade	
SOIL Fertile, free-draining	
HARDINESS Fully hardy	
FLOWERING Spring	

L | *Lonicera periclymenum* 'Serotina' Late Dutch honeysuckle

ALSO KNOWN AS WOODBINE, this honeysuckle comes from the deciduous form found in hedges and trees in the countryside. The flowers have dark red-purple markings and are noted for their strong evening scent. If space permits, also grow 'Belgica' (the early Dutch honeysuckle) with its red-streaked white flowers that open earlier in the season. Both like rich, moist but well-drained soil with shade at the base of the stem. When established, prune shoots back by one-third after flowering to keep it within bounds.

OTHER VARIETIES *L.* x *americana* (fragrant yellow flowers flushed red-purple); *L. etrusca* 'Superba' (smaller-growing, cream flowers turning orange); *L.* x *heckrottii* (flowers pink outside, yellow-orange inside).

PLANT PROFILE

HEIGHT 7m (22ft)

SITE Full sun or partial shade

SOIL Fertile, moist but free-draining

HARDINESS Fully hardy

FLOWERING Mid- and late summer

Lonicera x *tellmanniana* Honeysuckle

L

THIS CLIMBER IS SLIGHTLY DIFFERENT from some of the more rampant, vigorous honeysuckles because its deciduous growth is quite modest. Although they carry no fragrance, the flowers are such an attractive dark orange they are well worth growing for their colour alone. For the best show of flowers, plant it in light shade – although it also grows well in full sun – in cool, moist, free-draining soil. Prune established plants back by up to one-third to strong, young growth immediately after flowering.

OTHER VARIETIES *L. periclymenum* 'Belgica' (red-streaked white flowers, turning yellow); *L. tragophylla* (red-tinted, yellow or orange-yellow flowers).

PLANT PROFILE
HEIGHT 5m (15ft)
SITE Full sun or partial shade
SOIL Fertile, cool, moist but free-draining
HARDINESS Fully hardy
FLOWERING Late spring to midsummer

L

Lupinus arboreus Californian tree lupin

FOR THE MORE INFORMAL STYLE OF GARDEN, the Californian tree lupin makes an impressive, fast-growing, semi-evergreen shrub. It produces a rather sprawling mound of stems tipped by candle-like flowering spikes, each up to 30cm (12in) long. It requires quite specific conditions to do well, with light and sandy, quick-draining, reasonably fertile soil, and the type of mild, coastal, frost-free climate you'd typically find in California. An established tree lupin will provide useful shelter for other plants that dislike being buffeted by strong winds. Unfortunately, it is short-lived, so after three or four years it's worth taking cuttings to grow on to replace the parent plant, or allow it to self-seed and move the seedlings to where they are needed.

PLANT PROFILE

HEIGHT 2m (6ft)

SPREAD 2m (6ft)

SITE Full sun

SOIL Fertile, free-draining

HARDINESS Frost hardy

FLOWERING Late spring and summer

Lycium barbarum

L

NO MATTER HOW POOR YOUR SOIL, this quick-growing, often spiny, deciduous shrub will still shoot up to make a substantial hedge that will help protect a coastal garden from strong winds. Dry banks are another suitable site. Due to its scrambling and arching habit, it is not the neatest of shrubs, but you can keep it in shape by pruning it immediately after flowering. If you are growing it as a hedge, give it a hard prune in spring. Small clusters of purple to pink flowers appear in late spring and summer; the subsequent orange-red or yellow berries are glossy and small.

PLANT PROFILE

HEIGHT 3.5m (11ft) or more

SPREAD 5m (15ft)

SITE Full sun

SOIL Average, free-draining

HARDINESS Fully hardy

FLOWERING Late spring and summer

M

Magnolia stellata Star magnolia

ALTHOUGH SOME MAGNOLIAS make deciduous trees up to 10m (30ft) high, the star magnolia is a more manageable shrub. The unusual flowers, which open from blush pink buds on bare stems, look like white spiders up to 12cm (5in) across. If the flowers are damaged by frost, more will appear. This is one of the best feature plants going but it isn't scented (although if that's what you're after, there is a big choice of magnolias). The soil should be rich, moist but well drained and preferably acid, although it will tolerate the slightly alkaline. Prune for shape when young, then only to remove dead wood.

OTHER VARIETIES *M.* 'Betty' (cup-shaped, purple-red flowers, white insides); *M. globosa* (taller-growing, white flowers with red centres).

PLANT PROFILE
HEIGHT 3m (10ft)
SPREAD 4m (12ft)
SITE Full sun
SOIL Fertile, moist but free-draining
HARDINESS Fully hardy
FLOWERING Early and mid-spring

Although regular pruning is not required, overlong stems can be shortened in spring, after flowering, to a sideshoot or a whorl of foliage.

Mahonia x *media* 'Charity'

M

ONE GLANCE AT 'CHARITY' and it's easy to see why it has become so popular. A superb architectural plant with outward-pointing, dark evergreen, spiny leaves, it also produces dozens of long spikes of scented, yellow, winter flowers. Such a strong, tough, upright plant makes a highly attractive, impenetrable hedge. In general, mahonias prefer full or partial shade, but they will tolerate direct sunlight as long as the soil is not too dry. In the late afternoon winter sun the flowers look stunning. Prune only for shape after flowering.

OTHER VARIETIES *M.* x *media* 'Arthur Menzies' (lemon-yellow flowers); *M.* x *media* 'Buckland' (bright yellow flowers); *M.* x *media* 'Winter Sun' (densely clustered bright yellow flowers).

PLANT PROFILE		
HEIGHT 5m (15ft)		
SPREAD 4m (12ft)		
SITE Full or partial shade		
SOIL Fertile, moist but free-draining		
HARDINESS Fully hardy		
FLOWERING Late autumn to late winter		

BRACKET FUNGUS

Crab apples are prone to this fungus, which attacks most often in the autumn. Removing the bracts from the base of the shrub may slow its spread, but deterioration often continues inside the plant.

M | *Malus toringo* subsp. *sargentii* Crab apple

UNLIKE MOST CRAB APPLES, which are deciduous trees, this is more like a spreading shrub, being slightly wider than it is tall. Wild gardens will suit it best or, perhaps, the perimeters of a more formal garden. It isn't stretching the truth to say that it is sensational when in flower: the tightly furled, fat pink buds cover the stems and open to beautiful white blooms. These are followed by long-lasting, dark red fruit that decorate the branches from midsummer. It is not fussy about the soil conditions and will even tolerate a site in light shade.

PLANT PROFILE

HEIGHT 4m (12ft)

SPREAD 5m (15ft)

SITE Full sun or light shade

SOIL Average, moist but free-draining

HARDINESS Fully hardy

FLOWERING Late spring

Menziesia ciliicalyx var. *purpurea*

M

GIVEN ACID SOIL, this slow-growing, deciduous shrub is easy to please and will produce an attractive covering of small, dark purple-pink, urn-shaped flowers at the end of spring. Its compact size makes it perfect for the shady end of a border or a small woodland garden. One important thing to do at planting time is to incorporate plenty of organic matter into and around the planting hole because it must have moist, rich soil to do well. Throw in partial shade and shelter from cold winds and you're on to a winner.

OTHER VARIETY *M. ferruginea* (larger-growing, red-flushed yellow flowers, mid-green leaves turn red in autumn).

PLANT PROFILE
HEIGHT 1m (3ft)
SPREAD 1m (3ft)
SITE Partial shade
SOIL Acid, fertile, moist but free-draining
HARDINESS Fully hardy
FLOWERING Late spring and early summer

M | *Mimulus aurantiacus* Monkey flower

MULTI-BRANCHING AT THE BASE, with vertical stems, the monkey flower puts on a lavish, continuous show of blooms. In a range of strong oranges, yellows and dark reds, they are open, trumpet-shaped and nearly 5cm (2in) long with wavy edges (*see inset*). The soil is the most crucial factor and must be free-draining and rich; when this is coupled with a mild, sunny position flowers will be produced from late summer through to autumn. Plants are often short-lived, but by taking cuttings in early summer you can guarantee replacements.

OTHER VARIETIES *M. aurantiacus* var. *puniceus* (taller, brick-red to orange flowers, needs mild conditions); *M. longiflorus* (dark red, orange, lemon-yellow, or cream flowers with orange bands).

PLANT PROFILE	
HEIGHT 1m (3ft)	
SPREAD 1m (3ft)	
SITE Full sun	
SOIL Fertile, free-draining	
HARDINESS Frost hardy	
FLOWERING Late summer to autumn	

Mitraria coccinea

M

GIVEN THE RIGHT CONDITIONS, this scrambling South American evergreen shrub will put on a long-lasting show of glossy, dark green leaves and the richest red flowers. The buds start to open at the end of spring, with flowering continuing right through into early autumn. It's quite a fussy plant – although well worth the effort – needing a cool, mild, sheltered site on rich, acid soil that's moist but free draining. Ideally the roots should be in light shade and the top of the plant in sun. A wooded area or a partially shaded border is ideal. Lightly prune for shape in mid- to late spring.

PLANT PROFILE

HEIGHT 2m (6ft)

SITE Light shade

SOIL Acid, fertile, moist but free-draining

HARDINESS Borderline frost hardy

FLOWERING Late spring to autumn

M | *Myrica gale* Bog myrtle

WATERLOGGED, ACID SOIL … impossible conditions for most garden plants but perfect for bog myrtle. From mid-spring, this deciduous thicket-forming shrub bears clusters of gingery-coloured catkins among its long, dark green leaves. Plant it in groups along a well-used route through the garden, perhaps beside a wooded area. Having the plants close by means you can just reach out and crush a few of the leaves to enjoy their sweet aroma. *Myrica cerifera* (wax myrtle) grows three times as high as *M. gale* and, although it is not quite as hardy, it can be evergreen in mild winters.

PLANT PROFILE
HEIGHT 1.5m (5ft)
SPREAD 1.5m (5ft)
SITE Sun
SOIL Wet, fertile
HARDINESS Fully hardy
FLOWERING Mid- and late spring

Myrtus communis subsp. *tarentina* Common myrtle

M

BEING ONLY ABOUT HALF THE HEIGHT of its parent, *Myrtus communis*, this variety is a more manageable size and compact enough for most gardens. The evergreen leaves are aromatic when crushed and the pinkish-white flowers, and subsequent tiny white berries, put on a good show in mild and sheltered Mediterranean-style or courtyard gardens. Coming from the warm south, it needs excellent drainage, plenty of sun and protection from cold, drying winds. The longer and hotter the summer, the better the display of flowers will be.

OTHER VARIETIES *M. communis* subsp. *tarentina* 'Microphylla Variegata' (white-margined leaves); *M. lechleriana* (taller-growing, fragrant white flowers, aromatic red berries ripening to black).

PLANT PROFILE	
HEIGHT 1.5m (5ft)	
SPREAD 1.5m (5ft)	
SITE Full sun	
SOIL Moist but free-draining	
HARDINESS Frost hardy	
FLOWERING Mid- to late summer or early autumn	

N | *Nandina domestica* Heavenly bamboo

THE WORD 'BAMBOO' in this plant's common name is a misnomer – it's an evergreen or semi-evergreen shrub with bamboo-like stems and elegant foliage. The divided leaves are reddish-purple when young, maturing to green, then reverting to red again in late autumn (*see inset*). In midsummer, clusters of small, star-shaped flowers with yellow centres appear; in a warm season, they are followed by bright red berries. A sunny, sheltered site is essential, with moist but free-draining soil. If the winter is very cold, there is a risk it may not survive. Clip lightly for shape in mid-spring.

OTHER VARIETY *N. domestica* 'Fire Power' (smaller-growing, bright red leaves).

PLANT PROFILE	
HEIGHT 2m (6ft)	
SPREAD 1.5m (5m)	
SITE Full sun	
SOIL Moist but free-draining	
HARDINESS Frost hardy	
FLOWERING Midsummer	

Neillia thibetica

N

IN EARLY SUMMER, the gracefully zigzagging branches of this thicket-forming shrub hold clusters of small, rose-pink, tubular flowers (*see inset*) which, coupled with the bright green, lobed leaves, make a lasting impression. Such a broad spread makes it an unsuitable choice for a small urban garden but perfect for a woodland setting or a large shrub border. After flowering has finished, give it a light clip for shape. To renovate an established plant, cut one in four of the old flowered stems down to the ground to encourage new growth. Remove suckers in the autumn.

OTHER VARIETY *N. sinensis* (tubular, pinkish-white flowers, attractively jagged leaves).

PLANT PROFILE
HEIGHT 2m (6ft)
SPREAD 2m (6ft)
SITE Full sun or partial shade
SOIL Fertile, free-draining
HARDINESS Fully hardy
FLOWERING Early summer

O | *Oemleria cerasiformis* Indian plum

IF YOU HAVE ROOM IN YOUR GARDEN, be sure to include a female and male Indian plum from the western states of North America. The female shrub carries the distinctive small, black, plum-like fruit, while the male produces a better display of flowers. Both make a very dense thicket of upright growth which tends to arch towards the top. Stems are thickly covered in glossy, dark green leaves, while the clusters of small, white, bell-shaped flowers (*see inset*) are faintly almond scented. Another bonus is that, despite being deciduous, the Indian plum is one of the first plants to come into leaf in late winter. After flowering, cut back flowered shoots to strong new buds.

PLANT PROFILE
HEIGHT 2.5m (8ft) or more
SPREAD 4m (12ft)
SITE Sun or partial shade
SOIL Fertile, moist but free-draining
HARDINESS Fully hardy
FLOWERING Early spring

Olearia x *haastii* Daisy bush

O

THE APTLY NAMED DAISY BUSH really does produce a profusion of white, daisy-like flowers in summer. It is mostly grown in coastal gardens where it forms a salt-tolerant, sheltering, evergreen hedge. Prune it to shape as often as you wish because it will quickly throw up new growth. Other olearias aren't quite as hardy as this one, although the 3m (10ft) high *Olearia avicenniifolia*, and the 2m (6ft) high *O. nummulariifolia* (both scented) are suitable for mild areas. All need excellent drainage, though they are not fussy about soil.

OTHER VARIETIES *O. cheesemanii* (taller-growing, yellow–centred white flowers); *O.* 'Henry Travers' (lilac and purple flowers); *O. solandri* (very fragrant, pale yellow flowers).

PLANT PROFILE
HEIGHT 2m (6ft)
SPREAD 3m (10ft)
SITE Full sun
SOIL Average, free-draining
HARDINESS Fully hardy
FLOWERING Mid- and late summer

O | *Origanum* 'Kent Beauty' Oregano

THERE ARE MORE AROMATIC FORMS OF OREGANO than 'Kent Beauty'
– such as the pungent perennial *Origanum vulgare* – but few are as
attractive. Evergreen and shrubby, 'Kent Beauty' has trailing, ground-
hugging stems that are well suited to rock gardens or the tops of
dry-stone walls, where its stems can trail prettily down. From the
sunnier climes of the Mediterranean and south-west Asia, oreganos
won't survive saturating winter wet and instead must have free-
draining, even stony, soil with average fertility.

OTHER VARIETIES   *O. amanum* (bigger, pink flowers, green bracts
turning purple-pink); *O. laevigatum* 'Herrenhausen' (taller-growing,
purple-pink flowers); *O. rotundifolium* (pink flowers, lemon-green bracts).

PLANT PROFILE	
HEIGHT 10cm (4in)	
SPREAD 20cm (8in)	
SITE Full sun	
SOIL Average, free-draining	
HARDINESS Fully hardy	
FLOWERING Summer	

Osmanthus delavayi

O

THIS RICHLY SCENTED EVERGREEN SHRUB is equally useful as a border shrub or shapely hedge. It can even be clipped and styled as topiary, and the dark green leaves are beautifully glossy and leathery. Although the scented flowers are small, they appear in huge numbers; inedible, black, olive-like berries follow. Prune after flowering to keep the plant small or, at the other extreme, let it grow into a giant, white-flowering specimen. Give it a sunny, sheltered position on fertile, free-draining soil.

OTHER VARIETIES *O. x burkwoodii* (very fragrant white flowers, seldom produces fruit); *O. decorus* (larger leaves); *O. heterophyllus* (holly-like leaves); *O. heterophyllus* 'Gulftide' (smaller-growing, very spiny leaves).

PLANT PROFILE
HEIGHT 2–6m (6–20ft)
SPREAD 4m (12ft)
SITE Full sun or partial shade
SOIL Fertile, free-draining
HARDINESS Fully hardy
FLOWERING Mid- and late spring

O *Ozothamnus rosmarinifolius*

THE NAME OF THIS PLANT derives from the pungent, rosemary-like aroma of its leaves. It isn't a substitute for the herb, however, and neither is it quite as hardy. In cold-climate gardens it needs a sunny, sheltered position and a thick, protective mulch of compost to help it survive winter. From early summer, the strongly scented white flowers open from dense clusters of red buds. To create a more open, shapely plant, after flowering thin out a few stems.

OTHER VARIETIES *O. coralloides* (smaller-growing, yellowish-white flowers); *O. ledifolius* (smaller-growing, white flowers); *O. rosmarinifolius* 'Silver Jubilee' (silvery-grey leaves).

PLANT PROFILE	
HEIGHT 2–3m (6–10ft)	
SPREAD 1.5m (5ft)	
SITE Full sun	
SOIL Average, free-draining	
HARDINESS Frost hardy	
FLOWERING Early summer	

Paeonia delavayi var. *ludlowii* Tree peony

P

DECIDUOUS TREE PEONIES are an extraordinary sight and are on a much grander scale than their smaller perennial relatives. In spring, the stiff, vertical stems are covered in large, bright green leaves. The vivid yellow flowers, up to 12cm (5in) wide, open at the top of the stems. Other tree peonies are available, mainly in reds, purple-reds, maroons, salmon-pinks, and white, the widest choice coming from cultivars of *Paeonia suffruticosa*. Prune only for shape if necessary after flowering. Rich, moist but free-draining soil is preferred, with shelter from cold winds an essential.

OTHER VARIETIES *P. delavayi* (rich, dark red flowers); *P. tenuifolia* (smaller-growing, deep red flowers); *P. veitchii* (white or pink flowers).

PLANT PROFILE
HEIGHT 1.5m (5ft)
SPREAD 1.5m (5ft)
SITE Sun or partial shade
SOIL Fertile, moist but free-draining
HARDINESS Fully hardy
FLOWERING Late spring

P

Paliurus spina-christi Christ's thorn

CHRIST'S CROWN OF THORNS was reputedly fashioned from this striking, prickly shrub. The thorny shoots are vicious and if you want to protect your boundaries, this would make even the most determined burglar think twice about vaulting over. It is easy to grow, given full sun and well-drained soil – avoid heavy clay – in a mild, sheltered garden, and will soon make an impenetrable hedge. Star-like yellow flowers appear in summer and are followed by curious, flat, woody, disc-shaped fruit, 2.5cm (1in) wide. In autumn, the dark green leaves turn yellow before falling.

PLANT PROFILE

HEIGHT 4m (12ft)

SPREAD 3m (10ft)

SITE Full sun

SOIL Average, free-draining

HARDINESS Frost hardy

FLOWERING Summer

Parthenocissus quinquefolia Virginia creeper

P

A REAL POWERHOUSE OF A CLIMBER that will soon cover the walls of even a tall building. In autumn the leaves turn spectacular shades of red before falling (*see inset*). Self-clinging, it climbs by means of tiny suckers on the growing stems that latch on like limpets – bear in mind that, once in place, prising them off is impossible, so position your plant wisely. To cope with the weight of such a large plant, walls must be in good condition and trees should be large and mature. Stop growth 30cm (12in) below a roofline by cutting through the stems in spring.

OTHER VARIETIES *P. henryana* (shorter, white-veined green leaves); *P. tricuspidata* (taller, deeply toothed leaves turn brilliant red to purple).

PLANT PROFILE

HEIGHT 15m (50ft) or more

SITE Sun or shade

SOIL Fertile, free-draining

HARDINESS Fully hardy

FLOWERING Summer

P

Passiflora caerulea Blue passion flower

THE BLUE PASSION FLOWER from South America is one of the most exciting garden climbers. The exotic-looking flowers, up to 10cm (4in) across, look as though they belong in the jungle. In sheltered gardens flowering is prolific and may be followed, in hot summers, by orange-yellow, egg-shaped fruit. The quick-growing stems will spiral up a trellis, horizontal wires attached to a sunny wall or a hedge. Although it is an evergreen it will lose its leaves if the winters are cold and windy. Mulch with compost in winter to protect the roots, and cut stems back in early spring if you want to restrict its spread.

OTHER VARIETIES *P. caerulea* 'Constance Elliott' (all white flowers); *P. incarnata* (shorter-growing, pale purple flowers).

PLANT PROFILE

HEIGHT 10m (30ft) or more

SITE Full sun or partial shade

SOIL Moist but free-draining

HARDINESS Frost hardy

FLOWERING Summer to autumn

Penstemon fruticosus Shrubby penstemon

P

ALTHOUGH MOST PENSTEMONS are semi–evergreen perennials, *Penstemon fruticosus* counts as a small, evergreen shrub that is suitable for the front of a border or a rock garden. It spreads horizontally across the soil, putting down roots as it goes but there's no need for concern because it is easily controlled with secateurs. The lavender-purple flowers are typically funnel-shaped and, like all penstemons, it needs average, sharply drained soil in full sun.

OTHER VARIETIES *P. fruticosus* var. *scouleri* (deep purple flowers); *P. hirsutus* (taller, pale violet flowers); *P. isophyllus* (red to deep pink flowers); *P. pinifolius* (scarlet flowers); *P. rupicola* (shorter, deep red-pink flowers).

PLANT PROFILE
HEIGHT 40cm (16in)
SPREAD 40cm (16in)
SITE Full sun or partial shade
SOIL Average, very free-draining
HARDINESS Fully hardy
FLOWERING Late spring and early summer

P

Perovskia 'Blue Spire' Russian sage

PEROVSKIAS ARE EXTREMELY USEFUL plants because they flower at the end of summer. 'Blue Spire' catches the eye with its erect, multi-branching flower stems that bear more than a passing resemblance to lavender. The whole effect is wonderfully light and airy due to its finely dissected leaves which are the palest silver-grey. Although technically a shrub, it is best treated as a perennial and cut back to the lowest stems in spring to encourage vigorous new growth. It is not the least bit fussy and will grow successfully near the sea in average-to-dry, free-draining soil and also on chalky ground.

OTHER VARIETY *P. atriplicifolia* (violet-blue flowers, deeply cut grey-green leaves).

PLANT PROFILE
HEIGHT 1.2m (4ft)
SPREAD 1m (3ft)
SITE Full sun
SOIL Average, free-draining
HARDINESS Fully hardy
FLOWERING Late summer and early autumn

GREENWOOD CUTTING

In late spring, cut a non-flowering shoot and reduce it to 8cm (3in) with a straight cut below a leaf joint. Remove lower leaves and insert the cutting into a container of cuttings compost. Water with a fungicidal solution and place the container in a propagator. Once rooted, pot on the cutting.

Philadelphus coronarius 'Aureus' Mock orange

P

IF YOU WANT A HIGHLY SCENTED, DECIDUOUS SHRUB for a hedge or border, this is it. The exquisitely scented, creamy-white flowers of 'Aureus' open in midsummer on closely packed stems. The young leaves are golden-yellow in spring and summer, later turning green. To avoid leaf burn, choose a site in dappled shade. Unlike most mock oranges, this one will tolerate dryish soil. After flowering, cut one in four of the stems to the ground to promote new, bushy growth. Greenwood cuttings can be taken in spring (*see inset*).

OTHER VARIETIES *P. coronarius* 'Variegatus' (white flowers, white-margined leaves); *P. microphyllus* (smaller-growing, white flowers).

PLANT PROFILE	
HEIGHT 2.5m (8ft)	
SPREAD 1.5m (5ft)	
SITE Dappled shade	
SOIL Average, free-draining	
HARDINESS Fully hardy	
FLOWERING Summer	

P

Philadelphus 'Manteau d'Hermine' Mock orange

EVERY GARDEN NEEDS at least one richly scented, deciduous mock orange. Some are tall – 'Beauclerk' hits 2.5m (8ft) in height – while others are spreading – 'Belle Etoile' grows up to 2.5m (8ft) wide – but 'Manteau d'Hermine' is a more modest, wiry plant. It is not quite as richly scented as the first two, but the double flowers last slightly longer. Grow it in average, free-draining soil, and after flowering remove one in four of the stems to encourage new growth.

OTHER VARIETIES *P.* 'Innocence' (taller, single or semi-double, fragrant white flowers, yellow-mottled leaves); *P.* 'Sybille' (fragrant white and purple flowers); *P.* 'Virginal' (taller, fragrant, double white flowers).

PLANT PROFILE
HEIGHT 75cm (30in)
SPREAD 1.5m (5ft)
SITE Full sun or partial shade
SOIL Average, free-draining
HARDINESS Fully hardy
FLOWERING Early and midsummer

Phlomis fruticosa Jerusalem sage

P

IN THE FREE-DRAINING SOIL of a Mediterranean or gravel garden, Jerusalem sage will survive low temperatures, but in colder climates with damper soil it will need the protection of a warm, sunny wall. The evergreen, 10cm (4in) long, grey–green leaves provide plenty of substance and they contrast well with shrubs that have dark green foliage. From early summer, dark golden-yellow flowers appear at the top of the stems. Clip in spring or after flowering for shape.

OTHER VARIETIES *P. chrysophylla* (golden-yellow flowers); *P. italica* (lilac-pink flowers, woolly leaves); *P. purpurea* (purple to pink, sometimes white, flowers); *P. russeliana* (smaller-growing, pale yellow flowers).

PLANT PROFILE
HEIGHT 1m (3ft)
SPREAD 1.5m (5ft)
SITE Full sun
SOIL Free-draining
HARDINESS Fully hardy
FLOWERING Early and midsummer

P

Photinia x *fraseri* 'Red Robin'

AN EVERGREEN WITH A DIFFERENCE — at first glance, this beautiful plant's display of rich red, new spring leaves look just like flowers. 'Red Robin' is the best of the photinias for this effect, and with its neat shape it makes an extremely useful shrub for large borders, though it can also be grown as a hedge. Encourage bushiness and even more colourful spring foliage by pruning young plants in late winter. The small, white summer flowers are an extra bonus. Grow in fertile, moist but free-draining soil.

OTHER VARIETIES *P. davidiana* (dark green leaves turn red in autumn, red fruit); *P. davidiana* 'Palette' (slow-growing, creamy-white marked leaves); *P. davidiana* var. *undulata* 'Fructu Luteo' (yellow fruit).

PLANT PROFILE

HEIGHT 5m (15ft)

SPREAD 5m (15ft)

SITE Full sun or partial shade

SOIL Fertile, moist but free-draining

HARDINESS Frost hardy

FLOWERING Mid- and late spring

Phygelius x *rectus* 'African Queen'

P

PLANT PROFILE

FOR MOST OF THE SUMMER this exceptionally showy shrub throws up long spikes of small, dangling, orange-red tubular flowers. It's not reliably hardy and needs a sheltered, sunny spot in the garden, while fertile soil with excellent drainage is also a must. Although the foliage is evergreen, in cold winters the top-growth may die; don't worry if it does, just cut back stems hard and they should reshoot the following spring. In sheltered areas where the growth remains healthy over winter, lightly trim for shape in spring.

OTHER VARIETIES *P. aequalis* (smaller, dusky pink flowers with crimson and yellow); *P. aequalis* 'Yellow Trumpet' (creamy-yellow flowers, pale green leaves); *P. capensis* (yellow-throated orange flowers).

PLANT PROFILE
HEIGHT 1m (3ft)
SPREAD 1.2m (4ft)
SITE Full sun
SOIL Fertile, moist but free-draining
HARDINESS Frost hardy
FLOWERING Summer

P

Phyllostachys aureosulcata 'Aureocaulis' Bamboo

ONE OF THE BEST YELLOW-STEMMED bamboos 'Aureocaulis' offers extra colour from occasional green stripes. It makes a superb feature plant, hedge or screen. For a fun, lively combination, grow it against a beech hedge where in winter its green leaves will contrast well with the orange-brown beech foliage. It is an invasive type of bamboo and you must be ruthless in cutting out any shoots that appear where you don't want them – slice them off with a spade. Keep it well away from artificial ponds as new shoots may spear through the lining material.

OTHER VARIETY *P. bambusoides* 'Allgold' (golden-yellow canes, sometimes green striped, leaves occasionally yellow striped).

PLANT PROFILE

HEIGHT 3–6m (10–20ft)

SPREAD Indefinite

SITE Full sun or dappled shade

SOIL Fertile, moist but free-draining

HARDINESS Fully hardy

Physocarpus opulifolius 'Dart's Gold' Ninebark

P

THE YOUNG LEAVES OF 'DART'S GOLD' are a cheery sight in spring when they add a dash of bright yellow. In early summer, pink-tinged cup-shaped flowers are followed by tiny red fruit in autumn. Then in winter, the bark peels off in attractive curls. This deciduous shrub thrives in most well-drained soils – it does particularly well on acid, but results are likely to be disappointing on shallow chalk. Prune established plants after flowering, cutting one in four of the flowered shoots back to the ground.

PLANT PROFILE
HEIGHT 2m (6ft)
SPREAD 2.5m (8ft)
SITE Full sun or partial shade
SOIL Preferably acid, free-draining
HARDINESS Fully hardy
FLOWERING Early summer

P

Pieris 'Forest Flame'

AN EXCELLENT EVERGREEN SHRUB, 'Forest Flame' stands smartly
to attention, adding shape to any winter border. The glossy leaves
gradually fade from their late-winter livery of bright red, when
they make a strong contrast against the long sprays of white spring
flowers, and turn pink and creamy-white to end up dark green
in summer. Note that 'Forest Flame' must have an acid soil that is
fertile, moist but free-draining. It is not totally hardy, and in frost-
prone areas needs shelter from cold winds. To maintain a tidy
shape give it a gentle trim after flowering.

OTHER VARIETIES *P. formosa* var. *forrestii* 'Wakehurst' (brilliant red
young leaves); *P. japonica* (clusters of white flowers from late winter).

PLANT PROFILE
HEIGHT 4m (12ft)
SPREAD 2m (6ft)
SITE Full sun or partial shade
SOIL Acid, fertile, moist but free-draining
HARDINESS Frost hardy
FLOWERING Mid- and late spring

Pileostegia viburnoides

P

SELF-CLINGING WOODY STEMS enable this evergreen wall shrub to climb without being tied to a trellis or horizontal wires. An old, stout tree trunk also makes a perfect climbing frame. The shrub has unbelievably glossy, pointed, bright green leaves – up to 15cm (6in) long – that make a wonderful backdrop for the bright red berries of a cotoneaster or pyracantha. While *Pileostegia viburnoides* grows well in shade, a spot in full sun will encourage it to produce an abundance of broad sprays of tiny, white flowers. It also needs a sheltered site, and can be pruned lightly after flowering for shape and size, if required.

PLANT PROFILE

HEIGHT 6m (20ft)

SITE Sun or shade

SOIL Fertile, free-draining

HARDINESS Frost hardy

FLOWERING Late summer and autumn

P | *Piptanthus nepalensis* Evergreen laburnum

RIGHT AT THE START OF SUMMER, this semi–evergreen shrub is covered from top to toe in pea-like flowers. A slightly tender shrub, it will suffer if left to the mercy of cold winter winds, so choose a warm sheltered spot – the back of a sunny border or against a sun-facing wall are ideal. After flowering, cut back the flowered stems of wall-grown shrubs to within four buds of the base. When grown as a bush, in late winter prune it by about a third to create an open shape. It will make a sturdy support for climbers, such as clematis – strong blues and clear whites create a smart combination.

OTHER VARIETY *P. tomentosus* (pea-like, lemon-yellow flowers, followed by woolly seed pods).

PLANT PROFILE	
HEIGHT 2.5m (8ft)	
SPREAD 2m (6ft)	
SITE Full sun or partial shade	
SOIL Fertile, free-draining	
HARDINESS Frost hardy	
FLOWERING Late spring and early summer	

Most pittosporums grow naturally with a single, main stem, which makes them ideal for training as standards.

Pittosporum tenuifolium Kohuhu

P

VERGING ON A SMALL TREE, this shrub has black stems with glossy, wavy edged, fresh green leaves and, in late spring, dark red flowers that smell like honey. Initially narrow in shape, it later broadens out and makes an excellent hedging plant for a warm, sheltered garden in rich, moist but free-draining soil. In frost-prone areas you must provide protection against cold winds. Trim out damaged wood and clip for shape in spring – if you leave it until midsummer the shrub won't have time to recover before winter.

OTHER VARIETIES *P. tenuifolium* 'Silver Queen' (variegated leaves, dark red flowers); *P. tenuifolium* 'Tom Thumb' (shorter, bronze–purple leaves); *P. tenuifolium* 'Warnham Gold' (golden–yellow leaves).

PLANT PROFILE	
HEIGHT 4–10m (12–30ft)	
SPREAD 2–5m (6–15ft)	
SITE Full sun or partial shade	
SOIL Fertile, moist but free-draining	
HARDINESS Frost hardy	
FLOWERING Late spring and early summer	

P

Pleioblastus pygmaeus var. *distichus* Bamboo

TAKE CARE WITH THIS EVERGREEN BAMBOO. The height suggests it can be grown in a pot or tight space but it is much too invasive. In fact, the parent, *Pleioblastus pygmaeus*, is so rampant it quickly colonizes huge areas of ground. However, when used as ground cover in a wild garden this variety produces a lush and exotic effect, but don't site it near any plants you cherish because they will soon be swamped. Plant it in rich, moist but free-draining soil. In small gardens, try the more well behaved *P. auricomus*.

OTHER VARIETIES *P. humilis* (upright, dark green canes, mid-green leaves sometimes downy beneath); *P. variegatus* (shorter-growing, pale green canes with white nodes, dark green leaves with cream stripes).

PLANT PROFILE

HEIGHT 1m (3ft)

SPREAD 1.5m (5ft)

SITE Full sun or partial shade

SOIL Fertile, moist but free-draining

HARDINESS Fully hardy

Poncirus trifoliata Japanese bitter orange

P

NOTE THE COMMON NAME OF THIS DECIDUOUS SHRUB because, despite the luscious appearance of the fruit, it is bitter and inedible. This is a great shame because as a hardy, fruit-bearing shrub or tree it would be quite a catch. Still, its strongly scented, white spring flowers are exquisite and more than make up for this shortfall. In autumn, these are followed by the fruit, which, if the site is sunny and sheltered, will ripen from green to orange. Once the fruiting period has finished, you can prune it to any convenient size. It makes a magnificent ornamental hedge, which thanks to its long, vicious spines is impenetrable – so take care in gardens used by children. The soil should be rich and free-draining.

PLANT PROFILE
HEIGHT 5m (15ft)
SPREAD 5m (15ft)
SITE Full sun
SOIL Fertile, free-draining
HARDINESS Fully hardy
FLOWERING Late spring and early summer

P | *Potentilla fruticosa* 'Red Ace'

FOR GAPS, BORDERS, as a mini hedge or an edging plant, low-growing potentillas offer a great solution. They come in a wide range of colours, including white, pink, yellow, and red – 'Red Ace' is especially vibrant with yellow-backed petals – with single and double flowers. Their season is long, from late spring right through until mid-autumn, and they are low-maintenance, deciduous plants that are happy in free-draining, average soil. Prune potentillas lightly after flowering to keep them shapely.

OTHER VARIETIES *P. fruticosa* 'Abbotswood' (white flowers); *P. fruticosa* 'Longacre Variety' (lower-growing, bright yellow flowers); *P. fruticosa* 'Tangerine' (yellow flowers flushed with pale orange-red).

PLANT PROFILE

HEIGHT 90cm (36in)

SPREAD 90cm (36in)

SITE Full sun

SOIL Average, free-draining

HARDINESS Fully hardy

FLOWERING Late spring to mid-autumn

Prostanthera cuneata Alpine mint bush

P

A SUNNY, SHELTERED GARDEN that never gets too cold in winter is essential for this Australian evergreen. The safest place is in well-drained soil at the foot of a south-facing wall, where the plant can bask in the reflected warmth. It has strongly scented leaves and an arresting show of flowers that are delicately freckled inside with mauve and yellow. If you don't have a suitable spot in the garden, grow it in a large container and bring it under cover in the winter. Prune lightly after flowering to retain a neat shape.

OTHER VARIETIES *P. rotundifolia* (larger-growing, lilac-purple, bell-shaped flowers); *P. rotundifolia rosea* (light rose-pink flowers with mauve centres, grey-green leaves).

PLANT PROFILE	
HEIGHT 90cm (36in)	
SPREAD 90cm (36in)	
SITE Full sun	
SOIL Moist but free-draining	
HARDINESS Frost hardy	
FLOWERING Summer	

P

Prunus laurocerasus 'Otto Luyken' Cherry laurel

INDISPUTABLY ONE OF THE BEST CHERRY LAURELS. Although most of them are spring-flowering trees, 'Otto Luyken' is a small, dense, bushy shrub with glossy evergreen leaves that makes a perfect mini hedge. Spikes of white flowers appear in spring, often with a second flush in autumn. Prune to shape after flowering or at any time over summer, although there's a risk that you may sacrifice the autumn flowers. Very undemanding, it thrives in average, free-draining soil.

OTHER VARIETIES *P.* x *cistena* (taller-growing, white flowers, red-purple leaves); *P. laurocerasus* (taller-growing, fragrant white flowers, cherry-like red fruit); *P. laurocerasus* 'Rotundifolia' (taller-growing, good hedging); *P. spinosa* (taller-growing, white flowers, edible black fruit).

PLANT PROFILE

HEIGHT 1m (3ft)

SPREAD 1.5m (5ft)

SITE Full sun

SOIL Average, free-draining

HARDINESS Fully hardy

FLOWERING Mid- and late spring

Prunus tenella 'Fire Hill' Dwarf Russian almond

P

SMALL, UPRIGHT AND BUSHY, with many slender stems, 'Fire Hill' is an attractive mix of glossy, dark green leaves and, in spring, richly coloured, dark pink flowers. These are followed by grey-yellow fruit. Most deciduous ornamental cherries make extremely large shrubs or trees with sensational spring blossom and are far too large for the average garden, but 'Fire Hill' is just the right size. In autumn, before leaf fall, the foliage is injected with a dash of orange. It will grow happily in average, free-draining soil.

OTHER VARIETIES *P. glandulosa* 'Sinensis' (double pink flowers); *P. triloba* (taller-growing, solitary or paired pink flowers, red fruit).

PLANT PROFILE
HEIGHT 1.5m (5ft)
SPREAD 1.5m (5ft)
SITE Full sun
SOIL Average, free-draining
HARDINESS Fully hardy
FLOWERING Mid- and late spring

P | *Ptelea trifoliata* Hop tree

DESPITE ITS COMMON NAME, this is a deciduous shrub rather than a tree. However, it does make a large spread and, therefore, needs a correspondingly large garden. A woodland setting, perimeter border or a spare piece of ground are all ideal. Its three major assets are: first, the flowers are richly scented, as are the leaves when crushed; second, the star-like, greenish-white flowers are followed by winged, flattened, green fruit; and, third, the leaves turn a wonderful yellow before falling in autumn.

OTHER VARIETY *P. trifoliata* 'Aurea' (smaller-growing, bright yellow young leaves, turning green and then reverting to yellow in autumn).

PLANT PROFILE
HEIGHT 8m (25ft)
SPREAD 4m (12ft)
SITE Full sun or dappled shade
SOIL Fertile, free-draining
HARDINESS Fully hardy
FLOWERING Summer

Pyracantha 'Soleil d'Or' **Firethorn**

P

A PROLIFIC SHOW OF GOLDEN BERRIES is reason enough to grow this evergreen firethorn, but enjoy the show while it lasts because the berries are a favourite winter food of garden birds. Vicious thorns make pyracantha a good burglar deterrent, and it is often used as an impenetrable perimeter hedge or trained flat against the wall to encircle windows. Plants need protection from icy winds and prefer a free-draining soil. The best time to prune is mid-spring, even though this will reduce the amount of flowers and berries.

OTHER VARIETIES *P. coccinea* (taller, creamy-white flowers, scarlet berries); *P.* 'Golden Charmer' (bright orange-red berries); *P.* 'Mohave' (taller, red berries); *P.* 'Orange Glow' (dark orange berries).

PLANT PROFILE	
HEIGHT 3m (10ft)	
SPREAD 2.5m (8ft)	
SITE Full sun or partial shade	
SOIL Free-draining	
HARDINESS Fully hardy	
FLOWERING Early summer	

R

Rhamnus alaternus 'Argenteovariegata' Italian buckthorn

THIS EXCELLENT, FAST-GROWING EVERGREEN has plenty of yellow-green flowers and tiny red berries, ripening to black, but they don't compete with its major feature – the white-edged foliage. The leaf markings make a lively contrast with red-berrying shrubs, such as cotoneaster or pyracantha, and in an action-packed border they make a strong visual break between different colour schemes. Prune buckthorn lightly in early spring and remove any all-green leaves as soon as they appear or the whole plant may turn green.

OTHER VARIETIES *R. cathartica* (dark green leaves turning yellow in autumn, red fruit); *R. frangula* (dark green leaves turning red).

PLANT PROFILE
HEIGHT 5m (15ft)
SPREAD 4m (12ft)
SITE Full sun
SOIL Free-draining
HARDINESS Frost hardy
FLOWERING Late spring and early summer

Rhaphiolepis umbellata

R

SLOW-GROWING, WITH THICK, LEATHERY, glossy, dark green leaves, *Rhaphiolepis umbellata* makes an extremely versatile border shrub. At the end of spring it is liberally covered in clusters of small, star-shaped, scented flowers which are usually white but sometimes tinged rose-pink. Dark blue-black berries follow. Grow it in average soil that's relatively free draining, and position it in a sunny, sheltered site as it's not fully hardy. Clip for shape after flowering.

OTHER VARIETIES *R. x delacourii* 'Coates' Crimson' (dark pink flowers); *R. x delacourii* 'Enchantress' (dwarf, rose-pink flowers); *R. indica* (white flowers with pink-flushed centres).

PLANT PROFILE	
HEIGHT 1.5m (5ft)	
SPREAD 1.5m (5ft)	
SITE Full sun	
SOIL Average, moist but free-draining	
HARDINESS Frost hardy	
FLOWERING Early summer	

R *Rhodochiton atrosanguineus*

COLOURFUL AND CURIOUS, this unusual evergreen climber has dark purple, bell-shaped flowers with long maroon tubes (*see inset*). Given a sunny, sheltered spot it can be grown in the garden where it is usually treated as an annual. In a warm conservatory border it will safely overwinter as a perennial – just keep a look out for red spider mite and whitefly. Annual spring pruning at the base will force up fresh, vigorous growth. In the garden, you can train it up a pergola or a wall along horizontal wires, or over adjoining shrubs. Once the flowers open in summer they will keep coming until autumn, as long as the weather holds. Plants are easily raised from seed sown in spring in small pots on a windowsill.

PLANT PROFILE

HEIGHT 3m (10ft)

SITE Full sun

SOIL Fertile, moist but free-draining

HARDINESS Frost tender

FLOWERING Summer to autumn

Rhododendron luteum

R

IN SPRING, THIS EYE-CATCHING DECIDUOUS AZALEA fills the air with great wafts of honeysuckle-like scent. Given the right conditions – plenty of well-rotted organic matter forked into acid soil and bright sun – it is a real bonus in a woodland garden. It looks stunning against a dense carpet of bluebells with its flowers just starting to open on bare, twiggy branches. In autumn, the leaves turn red and orange before falling. Don't disturb the soil around the stem because it is shallow rooting.

OTHER VARIETIES *R.* 'Berryrose' (smaller-growing, apricot-orange flowers); *R.* 'Cecile' (smaller-growing, salmon-pink); *R.* 'Gibraltar' (smaller-growing, brilliant orange); *R.* 'Persil' (smaller-growing, white flowers).

PLANT PROFILE
HEIGHT 4m (12ft)
SPREAD 4m (12ft)
SITE Full sun
SOIL Acid, moist but free-draining
HARDINESS Fully hardy
FLOWERING Late spring and early summer

WATERING PROBLEMS

Although not all leaves will be affected, irregular watering can cause the foliage of rhododendrons to pucker and distort in this fashion. Leaf colour remains unchanged.

R

Rhododendron 'Vuyk's Scarlet'

BEAUTIFUL, COMPACT AND EVERGREEN, 'Vuyk's Scarlet' has crimson spring flowers and small, dark green leaves. Like all rhododendrons, it requires acid soil and plenty of leafy humus in its planting hole. You must also avoid planting it too deep because the roots like to grow just under the surface of the soil. Shade for part of the day is ideal, although this azalea will also grow well in full sun. If the stems of mature plants become tangled, cut them out, and to keep the plant neat, prune in early summer when flowering has finished.

OTHER VARIETIES *R.* 'Beethoven' (taller, magenta-pink flowers); *R.* 'Hinode-giri' (bright crimson); *R.* 'Hinomayo' (pink); *R.* 'Kirin' (deep pink to rose-pink); *R.* 'Vuyk's Rosyred' (rose, dark pink inside).

PLANT PROFILE	
HEIGHT 75cm (30in)	
SPREAD 1.2m (4ft)	
SITE Partial shade or full sun	
SOIL Acid, moist but free-draining	
HARDINESS Fully hardy	
FLOWERING Mid-spring	

Rhodotypos scandens

R

ALTHOUGH MODEST IN SIZE, this is a quality, vertical shrub suitable for medium-sized gardens. It has attractive leaves, about 6cm (2½in) long, that look like crinkled crisps. The papery, four-petalled white flowers appear from late spring (*see inset*), and are followed by glossy black berries. In ideal conditions, the flowers and berries will appear together. Grow this shrub in large borders or wild gardens, where its only requirement is decent drainage. Sun is best but light shade is perfectly acceptable. Give young plants a light trim after flowering, but prune established plants harder to reinvigorate them, removing about one in four of the stems.

PLANT PROFILE

HEIGHT 1.5m (5ft)

SPREAD 1.5m (5ft)

SITE Sun

SOIL Moist but free-draining

HARDINESS Fully hardy

FLOWERING Late spring and early summer

R | *Rhus typhina* 'Dissecta' Stag's horn sumach

DON'T CONFUSE THIS PLANT with its deciduous parent (*Rhus typhina*), which is a 5m (15ft) high tree. 'Dissecta' is shrubbier but has the same attractive, furry, reddish new shoots, followed by yellow-green flowers in summer. Its best season is autumn when it has clusters of plume-like, hairy crimson fruit, while the long dangling leaves, each one beautifully divided, turn arresting shades of orange-red before falling (*see inset*). It makes a colourful feature or informal perimeter shrub, and needs moist but free-draining soil.

OTHER VARIETIES   *R. aromatica* (shorter, leaves turn orange to red-purple); *R. copallina* (shorter, leaves turn bright red); *R. glabra* (leaves turn rich red); *R.* x *pulvinata* 'Red Autumn Lace' (leaves turn red-purple).

PLANT PROFILE		
HEIGHT 2m (6ft)		
SPREAD 3m (10ft)		
SITE Full sun		
SOIL Average, moist but free-draining		
HARDINESS Fully hardy		
FLOWERING Summer		

Ribes sanguineum 'King Edward VII' Flowering currant

R

DESPITE ITS TEMPTING COMMON NAME, this currant is ornamental and its tiny blue-black berries are inedible. The main attraction of this compact, deciduous shrub is the hanging clusters of dark red, tubular flowers which appear in spring. It's not very fussy and will thrive on average soil, as long as it's free draining. To retain a good shape, prune immediately after flowering, cutting any old, woody stems right back to the ground.

OTHER VARIETIES *R. sanguineum* (pink flowers, blue-black fruit); *R. sanguineum* 'Brocklebankii' (slow-growing, pale pink flowers, bright yellow leaves); *R. sanguineum* 'Tydeman's White' (taller-growing, white flowers); *R. speciosum* (dark red flowers, red fruit).

PLANT PROFILE

HEIGHT 2m (6ft)

SPREAD 2m (6ft)

SITE Full sun

SOIL Average, free-draining

HARDINESS Fully hardy

FLOWERING Spring

R | *Robinia hispida* Bristly locust

A COLOURFUL, DECIDUOUS SHRUB for poor, dry soils. Dark green leaves provide a perfect backdrop for the dangling clusters of rose-pink flowers that cover the arching stems in early summer. These are followed by prickly brown seed pods from which the bristly locust gets its name. Tie the fragile branches securely to horizontal wires fixed to a warm wall or fence as they can easily snap in strong winds. Alternatively, it will grow well as a border shrub in a very sheltered garden.

OTHER VARIETY *R. kelseyi* (smaller-growing, bright rose-pink flowers).

PLANT PROFILE

HEIGHT 2.5m (8ft)

SPREAD 3m (10ft)

SITE Full sun

SOIL Poor, dry, free-draining

HARDINESS Fully hardy

FLOWERING Late spring and early summer

Romneya coulteri Matilija poppy

R

THIS SURPRISE MEMBER OF THE POPPY FAMILY bears white, gently scented flowers with yellow centres that look like poached eggs (*see inset*) and appear over a long period. The deeply cut, grey–green leaves are also very attractive. The Matilija poppy has a reputation for being slow to take off, but it soon makes a substantial plant with new stems growing straight out of the ground. Choose a sunny, sheltered spot for it on rich, free-draining soil, and cover the crown of the plant with a thick mulch of compost over winter. If the stems get frosted, just cut them down to the ground in early spring and they'll soon grow back.

OTHER VARIETY *R. coulteri* 'White Cloud' (glaucous leaves).

PLANT PROFILE	
HEIGHT 1–2.5m (3–8ft)	
SPREAD Indefinite	
SITE Full sun	
SOIL Fertile, free-draining	
HARDINESS Frost hardy	
FLOWERING Summer	

APHID ATTACKS

Heavy infestations of these green, yellowish-green or pink aphids will reduce the quality of rose flowers. Many proprietary sprays are available to counter this problem.

R | *Rosa gallica* var. *officinalis* 'Versicolor' Rosa mundi rose

NAMED AFTER HENRY II'S MISTRESS, 'The Fair Rosamond', this small and showy, red-and-pink striped rose predates the 17th century. It belongs to a group of sweet-smelling, old garden roses called the Gallicas that flower only once in summer, although that display is nothing short of spectacular. Grow it as a single specimen or as a mini-hedge to inject colour into formal and informal schemes. A typical rose, it is a hungry feeder and craves rich, moist but free-draining soil. Prune only to reduce sideshoots by two-thirds, and over-long shoots by up to one-third.

OTHER VARIETIES *R.* 'Belle de Crécy' (taller, double, pink to purple flowers); *R.* 'Tuscany Superb' (double, crimson to maroon flowers).

PLANT PROFILE	
HEIGHT 80cm (32in)	
SPREAD 1m (3ft)	
SITE Full sun	
SOIL Fertile, moist but free-draining	
HARDINESS Fully hardy	
FLOWERING Summer	

Rosa 'Golden Showers' Rose

R

LIKE ALL CLIMBING ROSES, the scented, double-flowering 'Golden Showers' performs best when trained on horizontal wires fixed to a wall or grown around a pillar or post. This training forces new flowering growth along the main stems. If it is trained straight up, lower growth will be bare and flowers will be borne near the top of the plant. Climbers usually have stiff stems, and plants over three years old should by pruned by cutting back sideshoots by two-thirds after flowering. All roses prefer rich, moist but free-draining soil.

OTHER VARIETIES *R.* 'Gloire de Dijon' (taller, double, creamy-buff flowers); *R.* 'Guinée' (shorter, double, blackish-red flowers); *R.* 'Mermaid' (taller, single, primrose-yellow flowers).

PLANT PROFILE

HEIGHT 3m (10ft)

SITE Full sun or partial shade

SOIL Fertile, moist but free-draining

HARDINESS Fully hardy

FLOWERING Summer to autumn

R

Rosa moyesii 'Geranium' Rose

WHERE SPACE ALLOWS, *Rosa moyesii* 'Geranium' is one of the best of the flowering wild roses, although it is a little too large for a small garden. Its assets include fresh green leaves, outstanding, rich red flowers and large, orange-red hips (*see inset*). A growth habit that is smartly erect means it will keep to its allotted space in the border without sprawling over other plants. Virtually thornless, it also makes a beautiful ornamental hedge. Grow it in rich, moist but free-draining soil; restrict pruning to removing dead wood in spring.

OTHER VARIETIES *R.* 'Complicata' (single, pink flowers); *R. macrophylla* (taller-growing, single, fragrant, red flowers); *R. moyesii* (taller-growing, single, scarlet flowers).

PLANT PROFILE
HEIGHT 2.5m (8ft)
SPREAD 1.5m (5ft)
SITE Full sun
SOIL Fertile, moist but free-draining
HARDINESS Fully hardy
FLOWERING Summer

Rosa 'Nevada' Rose

R

FEW ROSES CAN RIVAL 'NEVADA' in early summer when its stems are covered with creamy-white flowers, each about 10cm (4in) across. Among the dense green leaves there are glimpses of vibrant reddish-brown arching stems. After deadheading the first flush of flowers, if the weather stays warm and sunny, a second sprinkling of buds will open in autumn. Once flowering has finally finished, prune the main stems by up to a third, and the sideshoots by a half to two-thirds. A rich, moist but free-draining soil suits it best.

OTHER VARIETIES *R.* 'Cerise Bouquet' (taller, semi-double, cherry-red flowers); *R.* 'Frühlingsgold' (semi-double, fragrant, pale yellow flowers); *R.* 'Scharlachglut' (taller, single, crimson-scarlet flowers).

PLANT PROFILE

HEIGHT 2.2m (7ft)

SPREAD 2.2m (7ft)

SITE Full sun

SOIL Fertile, moist but free-draining

HARDINESS Fully hardy

FLOWERING Early summer and autumn

BLIND SHOOTS

On any rose, shorten shoots without a terminal flower bud by about half, cutting to an outward-facing bud. These blind shoots divert the plant's energy if left unpruned.

R | *Rosa* 'Rambling Rector' Rose

RAMBLERS CAN BE GROWN IN TWO WAYS: you can let them clamber into a tree, eventually becoming a tangle of stems; or you can keep them tidy and more floriferous by growing them around a pillar or pergola. Either way, 'Rambling Rector' produces arching stems with small, sweetly scented flowers followed by red hips. Prune established plants after flowering, cutting one in three flowered stems back to the ground. Cut sideshoots back to two or four buds.

OTHER VARIETIES *R.* 'Bobbie James' (taller-growing, semi-double, fragrant, cream flowers); *R.* 'Crimson Shower' (smaller-growing, double, crimson flowers); *R.* 'Goldfinch' (smaller-growing, double, fragrant, deep yellow flowers); *R.* 'Veilchenblau' (double, fruit-scented, violet flowers).

PLANT PROFILE

HEIGHT 6m (20ft)

SITE Full sun

SOIL Fertile, moist but free-draining

HARDINESS Fully hardy

FLOWERING Summer

Rosa 'William Lobb' Rose

R

THIS ATTRACTIVE ROSE DOES A QUICK COLOUR CHANGE: the flowers open a deep purple and then, within 24 hours, turn lavender-grey, giving a striking two-tone effect. 'William Lobb' is a Moss rose, so called because of the furry growth that covers its graceful arching stems. Grow it in a sheltered border so that its sweet perfume will linger on the still air – close to the house against a sunny patio wall would be perfect. Plant it in fertile, moist but well-drained soil, and prune lightly immediately after flowering.

OTHER VARIETY *R.* 'Nuits de Young' (Moss rose, double, fragrant, maroon-purple flowers with yellow stamens).

PLANT PROFILE	
HEIGHT 2m (6ft)	
SPREAD 2m (6ft)	
SITE Full sun	
SOIL Fertile, moist but free-draining	
HARDINESS Fully hardy	
FLOWERING Summer	

R | *Rosmarinus officinalis* 'Severn Sea' Rosemary

ROSEMARIES SHOW GREAT VARIETY IN HABIT: there are upright ones that are ideal for hedging (such as 'Miss Jessopp's Upright'), while others are spreading and prostrate (such as 'Prostratus') and make surprisingly good ground cover. 'Severn Sea' veers towards a bushy type of growth, with arching branches, and it responds well to being gently pruned in spring to give it an open shape. All rosemaries like full sun, which intensifies the flavour of the leaves, and average, free-draining soil. If you don't regularly snip your rosemary for pot-pourris and cooking, then give it a gentle trim after flowering.

OTHER VARIETIES *R. officinalis* 'Roseus' (pink flowers); *R. officinalis* 'Tuscan Blue' (dark blue flowers).

PLANT PROFILE

HEIGHT 1m (3ft)

SPREAD 1m (3ft)

SITE Full sun

SOIL Average, free-draining

HARDINESS Frost hardy

FLOWERING Mid-spring to early summer

HARD PRUNING

Each year in summer, after flowering, cut all the flowered stems to the ground leaving only the young, white canes for winter display.

Rubus cockburnianus Bramble

R

MENTION THE WORD 'BRAMBLE' and gardeners visibly shudder, but this ornamental one is relatively tame. Still, it's most suitable for a wild or woodland garden where it will make a thicket of deciduous stems. In winter, the young, bare shoots are covered in a white, waxy powder, while in summer it produces tiny purple flowers followed by small, inedible berries. To encourage new white stems in winter, cut back all stems to within two or three buds of the base in early spring; alternatively, to retain some flowering stems, in summer cut down only those stems that have just bloomed.

PLANT PROFILE

HEIGHT 2.5m (8ft)

SPREAD 2.5m (8ft)

SITE Full sun

SOIL Average, free-draining

HARDINESS Fully hardy

FLOWERING Summer

R | *Rubus spectabilis* 'Olympic Double'

DECIDUOUS AND THICKET-FORMING, the beautiful, ornamental bramble 'Olympic Double' is grown for its 5cm (2in) wide purple-pink, double flowers. Opening in spring when the leaves appear, they are highly visible thanks to their fine colouring and the fact that the stems are still relatively bare. It is best grown in a wild or woodland garden and prefers average, free-draining soil. Prune after flowering, cutting back flowered shoots to vigorous buds. When established, also cut back about one in four of the old shoots to the base, forcing up new, vigorous growth.

OTHER VARIETIES *R.* 'Benenden' (rose-like, white flowers in late spring and early summer); *R. thibetanus* (red-purple flowers in summer).

PLANT PROFILE	
HEIGHT 2m (6ft)	
SPREAD 2m (6ft)	
SITE Full sun	
SOIL Average, free-draining	
HARDINESS Fully hardy	
FLOWERING Mid-spring	

Ruta graveolens 'Jackman's Blue' Common rue

R

THE SMALL, COMPACT LEAVES of this evergreen have a gorgeous blue tinge. Grow it at the foot of bright red and pastel roses or along the edge of a straight path where it will spill over to soften the hard lines, but do bear in mind that contact with the leaves can cause skin irritation. Many gardeners consider the pale yellow flowers to be a distraction and shear over the plant in spring to reduce their numbers. Because it needs sharp drainage and thrives in hot sites, the plant is suitable for growing in Mediterranean-style or gravel gardens. Rue is also frequently grown in herb gardens as herbalists use its leaves in various preparations, but it is poisonous if eaten.

OTHER VARIETY *R. graveolens* (taller-growing).

PLANT PROFILE
HEIGHT 60cm (24in)
SPREAD 75cm (30in)
SITE Full sun or partial shade
SOIL Free-draining
HARDINESS Fully hardy
FLOWERING Summer

S

Salix alba subsp. *vitellina* 'Britzensis' Willow

UNLIKE MANY WILLOWS that are grown for their impressive size, some reaching 15m (50ft), 'Britzensis' should be coppiced every one to three years to restrict its height and force up the beautiful, bright red new shoots that are its chief asset. The colour is particularly striking when seen against a clear blue winter's sky, and it should be positioned with this in mind. Cut the stems back hard in early spring, after the decorative yellow-green catkins have appeared, to produce a tracery of long, thin, almost vertical stems. For the best results, grow in rich, moist but well-drained soil.

PLANT PROFILE

HEIGHT 4m (12ft)

SPREAD 4m (12ft)

SITE Full sun

SOIL Fertile, moist but free-draining

HARDINESS Fully hardy

FLOWERING Early spring

Salix hastata 'Wehrhahnii' Willow

S

BARE, DARK PURPLE STEMS hung with a multitude of silver-grey catkins make this deciduous shrub an exciting addition to the early spring garden. When the leaves appear they are bright green. Unlike many tall-growing willows, this is a small shrub that is suitable for most gardens. To create a balance between old wood (bearing catkins) and new wood (giving the best-coloured stems), each year cut one in three stems to within two to three buds of the base. Grow in any moist soil, except shallow, chalky ground.

OTHER VARIETIES *S. caprea* 'Kilmarnock' (yellow-brown shoots, grey catkins); *S. fargesii* (glossy green shoots, slender green catkins); *S. lanata* (white woolly shoots, yellow catkins).

PLANT PROFILE	
HEIGHT 1m (3ft)	
SPREAD 1m (3ft)	
SITE Sun	
SOIL Moist but free-draining	
HARDINESS Fully hardy	
FLOWERING Early spring	

S

Salvia officinalis 'Purpurascens' Purple sage

AN ESSENTIAL PLANT FOR A SUNNY HERB GARDEN, sage is grown for its aromatic, evergreen leaves. For culinary purposes, one bushy plant is sufficient for even the keenest cook. The parent, *Salvia officinalis*, is a rather dull green but other varieties have good leaf colour and 'Purpurascens' is one of the best because its new foliage is an intense reddish-purple. Protect young plants in their first few winters – initially, pot up in autumn and bring indoors somewhere frost free. Free-draining soil and a sheltered site are essential.

OTHER VARIETIES *S. officinalis* 'Aurea' (purple-blue flowers, yellow leaves); *S. officinalis* 'Icterina' (yellow and green variegated leaves); *S. officinalis* 'Kew Gold' (golden yellow leaves flecked with green).

PLANT PROFILE	
HEIGHT 80cm (32in)	
SPREAD 90cm (36in)	
SITE Full sun to light shade	
SOIL Free-draining	
HARDINESS Fully hardy	
FLOWERING Early and midsummer	

Sambucus nigra 'Guincho Purple' Black elder

S

THE WILD GARDEN is the natural home for this deciduous elder. It is grown for the bracing colour contrast of tiny, pink-tinged white flowers against a backdrop of dark leaves, which are green in spring, turning blackish-purple and then red in autumn. The flowers are followed by tiny black berries which can be cooked and then eaten. For the best show of coloured leaves, cut all stems to the ground in winter or remove the old ones and prune the young stems in half. Elders grow well in most soils.

OTHER VARIETIES *S. nigra* 'Aurea' (yellow leaves on pink-flushed stalks); *S. nigra* f. *laciniata* (irregularly, finely cut leaflets); *S. racemosa* 'Sutherland Gold' (bronze young leaves turning golden yellow).

PLANT PROFILE
HEIGHT 6m (20ft)
SPREAD 6m (20ft)
SITE Full sun or partial shade
SOIL Average, moist but free-draining
HARDINESS Fully hardy
FLOWERING Early summer

S

Santolina chamaecyparissus Cotton lavender

THE FRONT OF THE BORDER is where this compact, mound-forming plant will make the greatest impact. Try planting it in rows as a low hedge to edge a path, or in a block that grows together to make very effective ground cover. In summer, button-like yellow flowers appear in great numbers (*see inset*), although some people prefer to shear them off so that they don't detract from the silvery-grey leaves and stems. The cool shades of cotton lavender make it a good gap filler for predominantly white borders.

OTHER VARIETIES *S. chamaecyparissus* 'Lemon Queen' (lemon-yellow flowers); *S. chamaecyparissus* 'Small-Ness' (dwarf, perfect for rockeries); *S. rosmarinifolia* subsp. *rosmarinifolia* 'Primrose Gem' (pale yellow flowers).

PLANT PROFILE

HEIGHT 50cm (20in)

SPREAD 90cm (36in)

SITE Full sun

SOIL Poor to average, free-draining

HARDINESS Frost hardy

FLOWERING Mid- and late summer

Sarcococca confusa Christmas box

S

A STRONG, SWEET SCENT IN MIDWINTER is the best reason to include this evergreen in the garden. The scented white flowers are followed by tiny black berries. Christmas box – so named because its leaves resemble those of *Buxus* (box) – is easily grown in average, free-draining soil, and will survive dry shade and a degree of neglect. Young plants grow well in containers – flank the front door with a matching pair in terracotta pots. Maintenance is minimal, just a spring pruning to maintain an attractive shape should suffice.

OTHER VARIETIES S. *hookeriana* (spreading, fragrant, white flowers, blue-black fruit); S. *hookeriana* var. *humilis* (smaller, fragrant, pink-white flowers, blue-black fruit); S. *ruscifolia* (smaller, dark red fruit).

PLANT PROFILE
HEIGHT 2m (6ft)
SPREAD 1m (3ft)
SITE Deep or partial shade
SOIL Average, moist but free-draining
HARDINESS Fully hardy
FLOWERING Winter

S

Sasa veitchii Bamboo

A MODERATELY INVASIVE BAMBOO, *Sasa veitchii*'s short, dense, leafy growth makes wonderful ground cover for wild and wooded areas of the garden. The dark green, glossy leaves develop distinctive white margins in winter, and are held horizontally from the purple-green canes. *Sasa veitchii* f. *minor* is worth tracking down as its slightly smaller leaves carry even stronger white margins and it is also markedly shorter. Both grow well in most ordinary soils, and to restrict their spread, you can plant them in an open-bottomed pit lined with paving stones.

OTHER VARIETY *S. palmata* f. *nebulosa* (larger-growing, purple-streaked canes, glossy bright green leaves with yellow midribs).

PLANT PROFILE

HEIGHT 1–1.2m (3–4ft)

SPREAD Indefinite

SITE Full sun to deep shade

SOIL Fertile, moist but free-draining

HARDINESS Fully hardy

Schizophragma hydrangeoides

S

SELF-CLINGING CLIMBERS, like this one, don't require horizontal wires or trellis to help them on their way; instead they need a sturdy, solid surface, such as a tree or wall, for their suckers to latch on to. *Schizophragma hydrangeoides* is a vigorous, deciduous climber with stems thickly cloaked in 15cm (6in) long, dark green leaves. In a sunny position it will produce masses of tiny white flowers in large sprays up to 25cm (10in) wide. Even if it is trained against a shady wall it will still throw out the odd spray. Prune in early spring by cutting back sideshoots to just three buds.

OTHER VARIETIES *S. hydrangeoides* 'Roseum' (white flowers with pink bracts); *S. integrifolium* (white flowers with creamy bracts).

PLANT PROFILE
HEIGHT 12m (40ft)
SITE Full sun or partial shade
SOIL Moist but free-draining
HARDINESS Fully hardy
FLOWERING Midsummer

S

Semiarundinaria fastuosa Narihira bamboo

TALL, MILITARY-STRAIGHT STEMS are typical of this type of bamboo. In cool climates, while it will almost always reach its full height, there's little risk of it spreading sideways and becoming invasive. Plant it as a dense but controllable perimeter screen (chop unwanted sections out with a spade), although if left unchecked, say in a wild garden, in time it will make impressive clumps or groves. When young, the thick, shiny canes are green with purple-brown stripes but as they age, especially if grown in full sun, the green is gradually lost. For best results, grow in rich, moist but free-draining soil.

OTHER VARIETIES *S. kagamiana* (shorter, good for clipping); *S. fastuosa* var. *viridis* (taller-growing, canes stay a lighter colour).

PLANT PROFILE
HEIGHT 7m (23ft)
SPREAD 2m (6ft)
SITE Full sun or light shade
SOIL Fertile, moist but free-draining
HARDINESS Fully hardy

Senecio viravira

S

A FIRST-RATE, SILVERY, EVERGREEN SHRUB with elegant, open growth and finely divided leaves. Some gardeners feel that the pale yellow, late-summer flowers detract from the plant's overall appearance and cut them off before they open. It is a popular foliage choice for white planting schemes. Because the plant is not reliably hardy, it needs a mild, sheltered position – for example, in a Mediterranean-style courtyard or against a sunny wall. Average soil is fine but it must be free draining.

OTHER VARIETIES *S. cineraria* 'Silver Dust' (lacy, near-white leaves); *S. cineraria* 'White Diamond' (oak-like, grey-white leaves).

PLANT PROFILE
HEIGHT 60cm (24in)
SPREAD 90cm (36in)
SITE Full sun
SOIL Average, free-draining
HARDINESS Frost hardy
FLOWERING Summer to autumn

S | *Shibataea kumasasa* Bamboo

THERE ARE MANY BAMBOOS available for small spaces and this non-invasive, clump-forming type can be clipped into a small, neat, leafy mound, or grown in a row to edge the front of a border or path. Its short-jointed, greenish-brown canes and rich green leaves will bring a welcome lushness to a gravel garden – during the summer, however, it will need regular watering. The foliage may become damaged during a severe winter but it will quickly recover the following spring. Unless you can replicate the conditions of its native habit in China and Japan, flowering is extremely rare: in Europe there was only a single recorded case in the 20th century.

PLANT PROFILE

HEIGHT 60–150cm (24–60in)

SPREAD 60cm (24in)

SITE Partial shade or full sun

SOIL Average, moist but free-draining

HARDINESS Fully hardy

Skimmia japonica 'Rubella'

S

INTERESTING THINGS start to happen to this plant in midwinter when the red-brown flower buds fatten up and by spring, you'll have a good show of tiny, white, scented flowers. 'Rubella' is a male plant and will not bear berries – plant a female skimmia close by for those – but the red-edged, dark green leaves provide year-round colour. As it can withstand the effects of both sea spray and city pollution, it is a very useful subject for hedging. Help plants along by giving them moist, rich, acid soil. Clip for shape after flowering, if necessary.

OTHER VARIETIES *S. japonica* (male and female, fragrant white flowers often pink-tinged, aromatic leaves); *S. japonica* 'Fragrans' (smaller-growing, free-flowering male); *S. japonica* 'Veitchii' (female form).

PLANT PROFILE	
HEIGHT 6m (20ft)	
SPREAD 6m (20ft)	
SITE Partial or full shade	
SOIL Acid, moist, fertile	
HARDINESS Fully hardy	
FLOWERING Spring	

S | *Solanum crispum* 'Glasnevin' Chilean potato tree

GIVEN SOMEWHERE TO SCRAMBLE, this evergreen or semi-evergreen climber quickly forms a mass of flowering stems. Yellow-centred, purple-blue flowers appear through summer and well into late autumn; these are followed by yellow-white berries. It looks stunning planted with a white or yellow clematis. Slightly tender, it prefers the warmth of a sunny wall and needs well-drained soil. To stop the stems from flopping forward or breaking in the wind, tie them to horizontal wires. If necessary, thin out stems in spring, and in cases of severe congestion cut back hard into the old wood.

OTHER VARIETIES *S. crispum* (lilac- to purple-blue flowers); *S. laciniatum* (smaller-growing, dark blue flowers, bright orange fruit).

PLANT PROFILE

HEIGHT 6m (20ft)

SITE Full sun

SOIL Free-draining

HARDINESS Frost hardy

FLOWERING Summer to autumn

Sophora microphylla 'Sun King'

S

ORIGINALLY FROM THE DRY VALLEYS of tropical regions, this evergreen shrub is equally happy in a woodland garden or sunny border; it also works well as a focal plant. Grown principally for its elegant leaves and dangling clusters of yellow, pea-like flowers, it makes a medium-sized, open bush. The flowers are long lasting and start to make their mark from late winter. Although hardy, 'Sun King' benefits from a warm, protected position in the garden, for example, at the base of a south-facing wall. The hotter the summer, the better the display of flowers is likely to be. Average, well-drained soil and a sunny position will ensure that this shrub thrives.

PLANT PROFILE	
HEIGHT 3m (10ft)	
SPREAD 3m (10ft)	
SITE Full sun	
SOIL Average, free-draining	
HARDINESS Fully hardy	
FLOWERING Late winter and early spring	

S | *Sorbaria sorbifolia*

A LARGE BORDER OR A WILD, WOODLAND GARDEN is the perfect home for this versatile, multi-stemmed plant. It makes an upright deciduous shrub with a spread that is almost twice that of its height. Exuberant white flower plumes (*see inset*) appear in summer above the ornamental foliage. When flowering is over, give the shrub a light all-over prune to help it retain a good shape; alternatively, in spring, cut back hard to near the base to encourage fresh new growth. Remove unwanted suckers to restrict the plant's spread. Tolerant of light shade, it grows best in rich, moist but free-draining soil.

OTHER VARIETIES *S. tomentosa* (taller-growing, white flowers, lance-shaped leaves); *S. tomentosa* var. *angustifolia* (taller-growing, red shoots).

PLANT PROFILE

HEIGHT 2m (6ft)

SPREAD 3m (10ft)

SITE Full sun to partial shade

SOIL Fertile, moist but free-draining

HARDINESS Fully hardy

FLOWERING Mid- and late summer

Sorbus reducta

S

MOST SORBUSES ARE TREES, renowned for their colourful berries
and autumn foliage, but *Sorbus reducta* is a multi-stemmed, suckering
shrub. Its size makes it ideal for a large shrub border, a wild garden
or woodland setting. In late spring, small white flowers appear,
followed by round, crimson berries that age to pinky-white. Before
falling in autumn, the glossy, dark green leaves turn glorious shades
of red and purple. Rich, free-draining, acid to neutral soil suits it
best but it will tolerate a range of conditions.

OTHER VARIETIES *S. cashmiriana* (taller-growing, white berries);
S. commixta (taller-growing, red berries, yellow to red autumn leaf
colour); *S. megalocarpa* (taller-growing, russet-brown berries).

PLANT PROFILE
HEIGHT 1–1.5m (3–5ft)
SPREAD 2m (6ft)
SITE Full sun or dappled shade
SOIL Acid to neutral, fertile, free-draining
HARDINESS Fully hardy
FLOWERING Late spring

S

Spartium junceum Broom

STIFF, VERTICAL BROOM IS A PLANT FOR ALL SEASONS. In winter it is covered with tiny evergreen leaves and then, from early summer through to autumn, these are joined by masses of fragrant, pea-like yellow flowers followed by long, dark brown seed pods. It is suitable for a shrub border and will also grow happily against a warm, sunny wall or fence. As long as it has well-drained soil, broom is extremely tough – it even thrives in exposed coastal gardens, and will also grow well on chalky soils. With age, if the shrub becomes too spindly, cut it back hard (but not into the oldest wood) to promote new, bushy growth.

PLANT PROFILE

HEIGHT 3m (10ft)

SPREAD 3m (10ft)

SITE Full sun

SOIL Fertile, free-draining

HARDINESS Frost hardy

FLOWERING Early summer to early autumn

Spiraea 'Arguta' Bridal wreath

S

IN SPRING, 'ARGUTA' ERUPTS into a mass of white flowers, making it an invaluable feature plant for a sunny border. It can also be included in a mixed hedge beside summer-flowering *Spiraea japonica*. Given an open, sunny position it will thrive in most gardens. After flowering, prune away old or spindly wood. When trimming a mixed spiraea hedge, bear in mind that spring-flowering types bloom on the previous year's growth and summer-flowering ones on the current year's growth.

OTHER VARIETIES *S. japonica* 'Anthony Waterer' (smaller-growing, dark pink flowers, leaves edged with creamy-white are bronze-red when young); *S. japonica* 'Little Princess' (ground cover, rose-pink flowers).

PLANT PROFILE
HEIGHT 2.5m (8ft)
SPREAD 2.5m (8ft)
SITE Full sun
SOIL Fertile, moist but free-draining
HARDINESS Fully hardy
FLOWERING Spring

S *Spiraea japonica* 'Anthony Waterer'

PRODUCING FLAT SPRAYS of dark pink flowers, up to 20cm (8in) across, this very popular deciduous shrub also features dark green leaves, often with a creamy-white margin. The young spring leaves are reddish-bronze. It is best grown as an informal hedge or in a shrub border, and will thrive in most garden situations as long as the extremes of wet and dry soil are avoided. After planting, give the stems a hard prune, reducing them to about 15cm (6in) above the ground. In future years, prune in the same way each spring, although for a permanent hedge you may prefer to prune less severely.

OTHER VARIETIES *S. japonica* 'Nana' (smaller, dark pink flowers); *S. japonica* 'Shirobana' (smaller, white and dark pink flowers on same plant).

PLANT PROFILE

HEIGHT 1.5m (5ft)

SPREAD 1.5m (5ft)

SITE Full sun

SOIL Fertile, moist but free-draining

HARDINESS Fully hardy

FLOWERING Mid- and late summer

Spiraea nipponica 'Snowmound'

S

PLENTY OF SPREADING SPACE IS REQUIRED for this fast-growing, deciduous shrub. Plan ahead when planting because just a few years down the line it will engulf anything in its path. In midsummer it puts on a wonderful show of flat, white flower sprays borne on arching branches. In spring, cut back spent flowering stems to strong buds; on established plants, cut back about a quarter of the old growth to the ground.

OTHER VARIETIES *S. japonica* (pink or white flowers); *S. nipponica* 'Halward's Silver' (smaller-growing); *S. thunbergii* (stalkless white flowers); *S.* x *vanhouttei* (smaller, compact, white flowers, diamond-shaped leaves).

PLANT PROFILE	
HEIGHT 1.2–2.5m (4–8ft)	
SPREAD 1.2–2.5m (4–8ft)	
SITE Full sun	
SOIL Fertile, moist but free-draining	
HARDINESS Fully hardy	
FLOWERING Midsummer	

S

Stachyurus praecox

AN UNUSUAL DECIDUOUS SHRUB for a woodland setting or growing against a wall, *Stachyurus praecox* is popular for its colourful stems and early flowers that will brighten up the late winter garden. Yellow buds form on its dark red–purple arching stems in autumn, then toward the end of winter, before the long, mid-green leaves appear, nodding rows of tiny, pale yellow-green flowers open. It's a breathtaking combination. Grow in rich, moist but well-drained acid soil and provide protection from cold drying winds. No regular pruning is necessary, just cut back for shape when necessary.

OTHER VARIETIES *S. chinensis* (bell-shaped, pale yellow flowers); *S.* 'Magpie' (smaller-growing, white leaf margins).

PLANT PROFILE

HEIGHT 1–4m (3–12ft)

SPREAD 3m (10ft)

SITE Partial shade

SOIL Preferably acid, fertile, moist but free-draining

HARDINESS Fully hardy

FLOWERING Late winter and early spring

Staphylea pinnata Bladdernut

S

IT'S A GREAT SHAME that this upright, deciduous shrub isn't more generally popular. It is at its best in late spring and early summer when drooping clusters of lightly scented, creamy-white flowers appear among the dark green leaves on its stout stems. Strange-looking, greenish-white, capsule-like berries follow in autumn. Bladdernut is an easy-care shrub that will grow in most gardens – average soil is fine as long as it never dries out. Clip it after flowering to keep it neat.

OTHER VARIETIES *S. colchica* (smaller-growing, fragrant white flowers, greenish-white berries); *S. holocarpa* 'Rosea' (larger-growing, pink flowers, bronze young leaves).

PLANT PROFILE

HEIGHT 5m (15ft)

SPREAD 5m (15ft)

SITE Full sun or partial shade

SOIL Average, moist

HARDINESS Fully hardy

FLOWERING Late spring and early summer

Stauntonia hexaphylla

THIS EVERGREEN WOODY CLIMBER from the Far East is a real talking point. Handsome, dark green leathery leaves, up to 15cm (6in) long, are carried on fast-growing twining stems. In spring it produces delicately scented, violet-tinged, white, bell-shaped flowers followed, after a long hot summer, by sausage-like, edible purple fruit, 5cm (2in) long or more – although you need male and female plants for pollination. If grown in a cool greenhouse border or conservatory it will climb to 10m (30ft); outdoors, in cooler garden conditions, growth will be more modest. Choose a sunny, sheltered site – against a south-facing wall is perfect – with free-draining, rich soil.

PLANT PROFILE

HEIGHT 10m (30ft)

SITE Full sun or partial shade

SOIL Fertile, free-draining

HARDINESS Frost hardy

FLOWERING Spring

Stephanandra incisa 'Crispa'

S

IF HIGHLY EFFECTIVE GROUND COVER is what you're looking for, then try this low-growing shrub which develops a dense, very wide-spreading thicket of deciduous stems. Interest extends all year round: greenish-white flowers open in early summer (*see inset*), and before falling in autumn the leaves turn a vibrant reddish-orange. Over winter the stems are an attractive, rich brown colour. The parent plant, *Stephanandra incisa*, is larger and makes a graceful 2m (6ft) high tree with a spread of 3m (10ft). Both plants require moist but free-draining soil and full sun or light shade.

OTHER VARIETY *S. tanakae* (taller-growing, yellow-green flowers, orange-brown shoots, mid-green leaves turning orange and yellow).

PLANT PROFILE

HEIGHT 60cm (24in)

SPREAD 3m (10ft)

SITE Full sun or partial shade

SOIL Moist but free-draining

HARDINESS Fully hardy

FLOWERING Early summer

S

Symphoricarpos albus var. *laevigatus* Snowberry

NO GUESSES HOW THE SNOWBERRY GOT ITS NAME. From autumn through to winter the arching stems of this deciduous shrub are weighted down with round, white berries. These are preceded in summer by pink, bell-shaped flowers that are a magnet for bees. The snowberry is a thicket-forming shrub that grows just about anywhere, tolerating exposed sites and poor soil. Use it in wild or woodland gardens or as a screening hedge. Tidy up plants every few years by thinning out congested stems in early spring.

OTHER VARIETIES *S.* x *chenaultii* 'Hancock' (low and spreading, white flowers, dark pink berries); *S.* x *doorenbosii* (pink-blushed white berries); *S. orbiculatus* 'Foliis Variegatis' (yellow-margined leaves).

PLANT PROFILE

HEIGHT 2m (6ft)

SPREAD 2m (6ft)

SITE Full sun or partial shade

SOIL Preferably fertile, free-draining

HARDINESS Fully hardy

FLOWERING Summer

Symplocos paniculata Sapphire berry

S

THE TWIGGY, DECIDUOUS SAPPHIRE BERRY grows into a large shrub or small tree that is suitable for sunny, sheltered gardens. At the end of spring it puts on an amazing show, with branches densely packed with delicately scented, small, star-shaped white flowers (*see inset*). You will only get to see the metallic-blue berries following a long, hot summer – another nearby plant for an exchange of pollen is essential, too. Slightly acidic soil is preferable, and it should also be rich and moist but free draining.

PLANT PROFILE
HEIGHT 5m (15ft)
SPREAD 5m (15ft)
SITE Full sun
SOIL Acid, fertile, moist but free-draining
HARDINESS Fully hardy
FLOWERING Late spring and early summer

S

Syringa vulgaris 'Charles Joly' Common lilac

MANY EXCELLENT, RICHLY SCENTED, deciduous lilacs are readily available which can make it difficult to select the right one. 'Charles Joly', with its sweetly scented, dark purple flowers, is one of the best spreading types. Grow it as a hedge, at the back of a border or as an individual specimen shrub. Best results will be achieved on rich, moist but free-draining soil. Deadhead the flower sprays as soon as they fade, otherwise they will spoil the look of the shrub, and then prune it after flowering.

OTHER VARIETIES *S. vulgaris* 'Firmament' (light blue flowers); *S. vulgaris* 'Madame Lemoine' (double white flowers); *S. vulgaris* 'Mrs Edward Harding' (double purple-red flowers).

PLANT PROFILE
HEIGHT 7m (23ft)
SPREAD 7m (23ft)
SITE Full sun
SOIL Fertile, moist but free-draining
HARDINESS Fully hardy
FLOWERING Late spring and early summer

Tamarix tetrandra Tamarisk

WITH MASSES OF THIN, SPINDLY STEMS almost completely covered in light pink flowers, this splendid shrub makes an arresting sight. It will struggle on anything other than very free-draining, preferably sandy soil – a coastal garden would suit it perfectly. After planting, cut the young plant back by half and then, in subsequent years, give it an annual pruning after flowering, cutting stems back to strong buds. As well as encouraging bushiness and maximum flowering, this treatment will also stop it becoming top heavy and falling over.

OTHER VARIETIES *T. parviflora* (larger-growing, purple shoots); *T. ramosissima* (larger-growing, red-brown shoots); *T. ramosissima* 'Pink Cascade' (rich pink flowers).

PLANT PROFILE
HEIGHT 3m (10ft)
SPREAD 3m (10ft)
SITE Full sun
SOIL Free-draining, sandy
HARDINESS Fully hardy
FLOWERING Mid- and late spring

T · *Tetrapanax papyrifer* Ricepaper plant

WITH ITS SHAPELY LEAVES, up to 50cm (20in) long, the ricepaper plant makes a striking, architectural statement in the garden. When young, the scaly leaves carry a powder-like covering; this quickly fades from the top surface, although it lingers on the underside of the leaf. White flowers appear in long woolly panicles in autumn and attract bees. These are followed by small, round black berries. If left unpruned, this suckering, thicket-forming evergreen will become leggy, but by cutting it hard back in early spring, to just 15cm (6in) above ground level, you will force up new, vigorous growth. Choose a sunny position sheltered from strong winds and hard frosts, which may kill it.

PLANT PROFILE

HEIGHT 5m (15ft)

SPREAD 5m (15ft)

SITE Full sun

SOIL Free-draining

HARDINESS Borderline frost hardy

FLOWERING Autumn

Teucrium fruticans Shrubby germander

T

SHORT AND BUSHY, this Mediterranean evergreen is worth growing for two reasons. First, it has aromatic, grey-green, silvery foliage, and second, it produces beautiful whorls of pale blue flowers (*see inset*). Its colouring makes it a good choice for pastel planting schemes where subtlety is called for. Some people find shrubby germander a rather untidy plant, but a light clip over for shape in spring will keep it in check. As it is not reliably hardy in areas where winters tend to be cold, it will need a sheltered site. Plant it in free-draining soil; avoid heavy clay at all costs.

OTHER VARIETIES *T. polium* (smaller, purple or yellow flowers, white-woolly, grey-green leaves); *T. subspinosum* (smaller, pink flowers, spiny).

PLANT PROFILE

HEIGHT 60–100cm (24–39in)

SPREAD 4m (12ft)

SITE Full sun

SOIL Free-draining

HARDINESS Frost hardy

FLOWERING Summer

Thymus 'Doone Valley' Thyme

THE DARK GREEN LEAVES OF THIS EVERGREEN thyme are distinctly marked with vibrant yellow spots, but it has only the faintest scent of lemon. Rather than planting it in the herb garden, it is better used in a rock garden or to fill gaps in a terrace where it will thrive in the free-draining, poor soil and the reflected heat from the paving. A gentle trim after flowering is all that is needed to keep it shapely and to encourage bushiness.

OTHER VARIETIES *T. x citriodorus* 'Golden King' (taller-growing, gold-margined leaves); *T. herba-barona* (smaller-growing, pink flowers); *T. vulgaris* (taller-growing, purple to white flowers, aromatic leaves).

PLANT PROFILE	
HEIGHT	12cm (5in)
SPREAD	35cm (14in)
SITE	Full sun
SOIL	Poor, free-draining
HARDINESS	Fully hardy
FLOWERING	Summer

Trachelospermum jasminoides Star jasmine

T

TWISTING, TWINING AND DELICATELY SCENTED, this evergreen climber will happily grow through support plants, such as holly, or it can be tied to wires and grown up a sunny, sheltered wall, or trained over a pergola. It goes particularly well with red and yellow roses or clematis. From midsummer it produces white flowers, while in winter its large, glossy green leaves turn reddish-bronze. Given full sun and good drainage (so that the soil is never waterlogged) it makes an exotic plant for a sheltered garden. Prune lightly immediately after flowering, or in spring if it is outgrowing its allotted space.

OTHER VARIETY *T. asiaticum* (shorter-growing, fragrant creamy-white flowers ageing to yellow).

PLANT PROFILE

HEIGHT 9m (28ft)

SITE Full sun or partial shade

SOIL Free-draining, fertile

HARDINESS Frost hardy

FLOWERING Mid- and late summer

T

Trachycarpus fortunei Chusan palm

IN TIME, THE CHUSAN PALM WILL BECOME A GIANT – a tall slender trunk topped with a crown of leaves. It is, however, slow growing and initially quite shrubby. The fan-shaped leaves are the main focus, reaching up to 75cm (30in) long, and make a particularly attractive feature next to the vertical, strap-like leaves of *Phormium tenax* (New Zealand flax). In its first few years this palm is slightly tender and needs protection over winter – packing straw around the crown provides good insulation – and shelter from the damaging effects of cold winds. Long, pendent spikes of yellow flowers appear in early summer followed, on female plants, by blue-black fruit.

PLANT PROFILE

HEIGHT 20m (70ft)

SPREAD 2.5m (8ft)

SITE Full sun or light shade

SOIL Fertile, free-draining

HARDINESS Frost hardy

FLOWERING Early summer

Tropaeolum speciosum Flame nasturtium

T

THERE SHOULD BE ROOM in most gardens for at least one of these climbers from South America. It sends up a mass of slender stems in early summer bearing rich red flowers that look particularly fine when trained through other climbers or dark green hedges, and over adjacent shrubs. Provide neutral to acid, moist, rich soil, and a position where the roots are in the shade and the flowers in the sun. When the plant dies back in autumn, remove all the top-growth and cover it with a protective mulch of compost.

OTHER VARIETIES *T. majus* 'Hermine Grashoff' (double, bright red flowers); *T. tuberosum* (orange and yellow flowers, veined with brown); *T. tuberosum* var. *lineamaculatum* 'Ken Aslet' (orange flowers).

PLANT PROFILE

HEIGHT 3m (10ft)

SITE Full sun or partial shade

SOIL Moist, fertile

HARDINESS Frost hardy

FLOWERING Summer to autumn

U | *Ulex europaeus* Gorse

FLASHY AND YELLOW FLOWERED, this evergreen shrub is suitable for poor, acid to neutral soils. The main show of colour comes in the second half of spring, but it will then continue to flower intermittently throughout the year. Gorse is a densely twiggy, spine-packed shrub with dark brown seed pods that appear in summer – on hot sunny days they open with a loud crack. Grow it in a wild garden or on a dry, sunny slope. Every two or three years after flowering give it an all-over prune to keep it in shape.

OTHER VARIETIES *U. europaeus* 'Flore Pleno' (slightly more compact, double flowers); *U. gallii* (smaller-growing, pea-like, bright yellow flowers, spine-tipped green shoots).

PLANT PROFILE	
HEIGHT To 2.5m (8ft)	
SPREAD 2m (6ft)	
SITE Full sun	
SOIL Poor, free-draining	
HARDINESS Fully hardy	
FLOWERING Second half of spring and later	

Vaccinium glaucoalbum Bilberry

V

THIS SUCKERING EVERGREEN SHRUB makes a dense thicket of stiff, broad, dark green leaves with white undersides. The pale pink flowers open at the end of spring and are followed by tiny, blue-black, white-bloomed, edible berries that last into winter. It is a strikingly attractive shrub with just one drawback – it is not entirely hardy and needs a sunny, sheltered site. The soil should be acid, peaty or sandy, and free draining but moist. A light trim after it has flowered will keep it in good shape.

OTHER VARIETIES *V. corymbosum* (larger-growing, white flowers, edible blue-black berries); *V. nummularia* (smaller-growing, red-tipped pink flowers); *V. ovatum* (larger-growing, pink-flushed white flowers).

PLANT PROFILE

HEIGHT 50–120cm (20–48in)

SPREAD 1m (3ft)

SITE Full sun or partial shade

SOIL Acid, moist but free-draining

HARDINESS Frost hardy

FLOWERING Late spring and early summer

THINNING OUT STEMS

Young plants should not be pruned at all. With established plants, remove up to one in five stems right back to ground level to prevent congestion.

V

Viburnum x *bodnantense* 'Dawn'

WITH ITS STRONG SCENT wafting around on still days, this plant is a must for the winter garden. The upward-pointing woody stems are bare at this time of year, save for small clusters of tiny pink flowers that age to white. These appear over a long period from late autumn to spring. *Viburnum* x *burkwoodii,* which flowers in spring, has the bonus of dark green, glossy, semi-evergreen leaves. Both thrive in average, free-draining soil, and can be pruned lightly after flowering.

OTHER VARIETIES *V.* x *bodnantense* 'Charles Lamont' (bright pink flowers); *V.* x *burkwoodii* 'Anne Russell' (white fragrant flowers, compact); *V.* x *burkwoodii* 'Park Farm Hybrid' (dark pink flowers ageing to white, leaves turn orange and red in autumn).

PLANT PROFILE

HEIGHT 3m (10ft)

SPREAD 2m (6ft)

SITE Full sun or partial shade

SOIL Average, free-draining

HARDINESS Fully hardy

FLOWERING Late autumn to spring

Viburnum opulus 'Compactum' Guelder rose

V

THE DECIDUOUS PARENT PLANT, *Viburnum opulus,* and its many cultivars grow vigorously and make huge bushes, but 'Compactum' is different being slow growing and, as its name suggests, quite compact. In early summer it produces flat sprays of white flowers followed, in autumn, by bright red berries (*see inset*). At this time of year the leaves also turn red before falling. In damp winter weather the plant may give off an unpleasant smell but that's a small price to pay for such beauty. Prune out older stems after flowering to allow new growth to regenerate the bush.

OTHER VARIETY *V. opulus* 'Roseum' (white flowers, sometimes green-tinted, purple-tinted leaves in autumn).

PLANT PROFILE
HEIGHT 1.5m (5ft)
SPREAD 1.5m (5ft)
SITE Full sun or partial shade
SOIL Fertile, moist but free-draining
HARDINESS Fully hardy
FLOWERING Late spring and early summer

Viburnum plicatum 'Mariesii' Wedding cake tree

THINK OF A DECIDUOUS BUSH WITH TIERED, horizontal branches covered in white flowers (*see inset*), and this plant's common name starts to make sense. The flowers are highlighted by dark green leaves which, by autumn, turn attractive shades of pink and purple. Such a vigorous shrub needs to go in a large border or a wild or woodland garden. 'Mariesii' thrives in most soils, provided they are well drained and fairly fertile. In gardens with heavy clay, grow it at the top of a bank where the drainage is much better.

OTHER VARIETIES *V. plicatum* 'Grandiflorum' (large heads of white flowers); *V. plicatum* 'Pink Beauty' (white flowers ageing to pink); *V. plicatum* 'Rowallene' (compact, red–purple autumn leaves, red fruit).

PLANT PROFILE	
HEIGHT 3m (10ft)	
SPREAD 4m (12ft)	
SITE Sun or semi-shade	
SOIL Fertile, free-draining	
HARDINESS Fully hardy	
FLOWERING Late spring	

STANDARDS

Viburnums tend to make new growth low down on the main stem. To train them as standards, rub out new shoots on the trunk as they appear.

Viburnum tinus Laurustinus

V

EASILY GROWN AND RELIABLE, this evergreen provides a compact bush of dark green leaves and reddish twigs. The main attraction begins in late autumn when the flower buds start to fatten, and in mild spells they open to give a fine show of blooms from midwinter (later in colder areas) that continues well into spring. Blue-black fruit follows. This shrub does best in moist but free-draining soil.

OTHER VARIETIES *V. tinus* 'Gwenllian' (pink-tinged white flowers); *V. tinus* 'Pink Prelude' (white flowers ageing to pink from pink buds); *V. tinus* 'Purpureum' (young bronze foliage); *V. tinus* 'Variegatum' (leaves margined with creamy-yellow).

PLANT PROFILE

HEIGHT 3m (10ft)

SPREAD 3m (10ft)

SITE Full sun or partial shade

SOIL Moist but free-draining

HARDINESS Fully hardy

FLOWERING Late winter to spring

V | *Vitis coignetiae* Crimson glory vine

ONE OF THE MOST SPECTACULAR AUTUMN DISPLAYS of any climber is provided by this plant when its large, lobed leaves turn shades of red, yellow, and orange before falling. Make sure you have enough room for its prodigious growth, and ensure that the stems don't encroach on to a roof and dislodge tiles. Stout trees and large pergolas make good alternative climbing frames – excess growth can be removed in midwinter and midsummer. Given plenty of warmth and sun, tiny green flowers are followed by small, black (inedible) grapes. Provide a free-draining, rich soil.

OTHER VARIETY *V.* 'Brant' (bronze-red autumn leaves, edible blue-black grapes).

PLANT PROFILE

HEIGHT 15m (50ft)

SITE Full sun

SOIL Fertile, free-draining

HARDINESS Fully hardy

FLOWERING Summer

Weigela 'Looymansii Aurea'

W

PERK UP LATE-SPRING GARDENS with this slow-growing, rounded, deciduous shrub which combines an abundant show of bell-shaped pink flowers with arching stems of golden-yellow leaves. Pruning involves cutting flowered shoots back to a vigorous bud as soon as the flowers fade. When the plant is mature, cut about a quarter of the old stems back to the base annually. For best results, plant it in free-draining, rich soil.

OTHER VARIETIES *W.* 'Abel Carrière' (larger-growing, dark pink-red flowers with yellow-spotted throats); *W.* 'Bristol Ruby' (larger-growing, dark red flowers); *W.* 'Praecox Variegata' (creamy-yellow margined leaves).

PLANT PROFILE
HEIGHT 1.5m (5ft)
SPREAD 1.5m (5ft)
SITE Partial shade
SOIL Fertile, free-draining
HARDINESS Fully hardy
FLOWERING Late spring and early summer

W | *Wisteria floribunda* 'Multijuga'

THERE ARE TWO TYPES OF WISTERIA: Chinese (*Wisteria sinensis*) and Japanese (*W. floribunda*). Chinese types are more popular because they generally climb higher, and have larger flowers with a stronger scent. However, they flower in late spring when their whole crop of blooms can be caught by frost. 'Multijuga' is useful because the flowers of this Japanese type open later, at the start of summer, when its long, pendent flowering stems can reach up to 1.2m (4ft). Grow it in free-draining, well-watered soil against a wall or up a sturdy tree.

OTHER VARIETIES *W. floribunda* 'Alba' (white flowers); *W. floribunda* 'Rosea' (pink flowers).

PLANT PROFILE

HEIGHT 9m (28ft) or more

SITE Full sun or partial shade

SOIL Moist but free-draining

HARDINESS Fully hardy

FLOWERING Early summer

Xanthoceras sorbifolium

X

WHY THIS DELIGHTFUL, DECIDUOUS CHINESE SHRUB isn't a more common site in gardens is a mystery. Its native habitat of scrubby areas and woodland edge makes it an easy plant to grow. It will thrive in a large border or woodland garden if given fertile, free-draining soil and plenty of sun. The star-shaped, lightly scented white flowers coincide with the appearance of its new leaves. The flowers have contrasting dark red centres, and the leaves start off pale green but gradually become darker as they mature. It is completely hardy, and should be pruned after flowering.

PLANT PROFILE	
HEIGHT	4m (12ft)
SPREAD	3m (10ft)
SITE	Full sun
SOIL	Fertile, free-draining
HARDINESS	Fully hardy
FLOWERING	Late spring

Y

Yucca filamentosa 'Bright Edge' **Adam's needle**

STRIPED GREEN AND YELLOW, the sword-like leaves erupt out of the ground making 'Bright Edge' a top-quality architectural plant. Just watch out for the needle-like spines on the leaf tips. In summer it sends up sturdy 2m (6ft) spikes packed with lightly scented, white flowers. Since excellent drainage is a necessity, it grows best in free-draining soil in a Mediterranean-style garden or on a sunny bank. It will also appreciate the sharp drainage in a large pot. Create a mixed yucca display with the frost-hardy *Yucca whipplei* and *Y. gloriosa*.

OTHER VARIETIES *Y. filamentosa* 'Variegata' (white-margined, blue-green leaves); *Y. flaccida* 'Golden Sword' (yellow-margined leaves); *Y. flaccida* 'Ivory' (creamy-white flowers).

PLANT PROFILE
HEIGHT 75cm (30in)
SPREAD 1.5m (5ft)
SITE Full sun
SOIL Free-draining
HARDINESS Fully hardy
FLOWERING Mid- and late summer

Yushania anceps 'Pitt White' Bamboo

Y

THIS HIGHLY INVASIVE, EVERGREEN BAMBOO from India has glossy
deep green canes that initially shoot bolt upright. In time, however,
they arch over under the weight of the leaves which can reach up
to 14cm (5½in) long. Don't even think about growing a plant as
vigorous as this in a small garden, but where space allows exploit
its rampant tendencies and use it as a perimeter hedge or screen, or
as a specimen plant for a wild garden where you can work around
the plant to dig out any excess growth. Ideally, this bamboo needs
rich, moist but free-draining soil, and a sheltered spot out of cold
winter winds which may damage the leaves.

PLANT PROFILE

HEIGHT 4m (12ft)

SPREAD Indefinite

SITE Full sun or
partial shade

SOIL Moist, fertile,
free-draining

HARDINESS Fully hardy

Z | *Zanthoxylum piperitum* Japan pepper

ALTHOUGH THE FLOWERS ARE INSIGNIFICANT, this deciduous, spiny bush has very attractive foliage with 15cm (6in) long, glossy, dark green leaves that turn yellow in autumn. Tear up a leaf and it will immediately release a strong, aromatic scent. The small, early summer flowers are followed by tiny red berries that split open to reveal black seeds. Bite into one and you will instantly detect a peppery heat, and they are, in fact, used as a pepper substitute in Japan. It will grow in most gardens but must have free-draining, fertile soil.

OTHER VARIETY   *Z. simulans* (larger-growing, warty red fruit, large, glossy dark green leaves turning reddish-yellow in autumn).

PLANT PROFILE
HEIGHT 2.5m (8ft)
SPREAD 2.5m (8ft)
SITE Full sun or light shade
SOIL Fertile, free-draining
HARDINESS Fully hardy
FLOWERING Early summer

Zenobia pulverulenta

Z

AN UNDERRATED SHRUB, zenobia mixes well with rhododendrons, enjoying the same acid, moist, rich soil. Over the course of the year it is quite colourful with young leaves that carry a blue tinge before turning deep, glossy green, followed by clusters of dainty, bell-shaped, scented white flowers which appear in early summer. In autumn, it puts on a magnificent display when its leaves redden before falling. There are two pruning regimes to follow: give it a medium trim after flowering has finished, cutting back to vigorous buds; then, every four years, be more severe, cutting it back close to the base to force up strong, new, vigorous growth.

PLANT PROFILE

HEIGHT 2m (6ft)

SPREAD 1.5m (5ft)

SITE Sun or partial shade

SOIL Acid, moist, fertile

HARDINESS Fully hardy

FLOWERING Early and midsummer

The publisher would like to thank the following for their kind permission to reproduce their photographs:

a=above; c=centre; b=below; l=left; r=right t=top;

A-Z Botanical Collection:
45c, 227c, 257tr; Ailsa Allaby 212c; Chris Martin Bahr 214c; Pam Collins 197c; Ian Gowland 79tr; Matt Johnston 236c; Nina McKenna 193c; Elsa M. Megson 257c; Maurice Nimmo 33c, 207c; Malcolm Richards 110c; J.Malcolm Smith 270c; Adrian Thomas 184c, 297tr; A.Young 296c

Garden Picture Library: .
Brian Carter 275c; John Glover 7tr, 216tr, 216c; Neil Holmes 156c, 313c; Howard Rice 6l, 79c

Garden World Images:
7br

Andrew Lawson:
2c, 288c

Clive Nichols:
304c; Hadspen garden, Somerset 63tr

Photos Horticultural:
28c, 38c, 39c, 40c, 50c, 55c, 60c, 63c, 68c, 71c, 77c, 89c, 91c, 100c, 120c, 121c, 122C, 134c, 151c, 164c, 241c, 245c, 249c, 255c, 264c, 295c, 297c

Plant Pictures World Wide:
29c, 44c

Roger Smith/DK:
14c, 27c, 35c, 59c, 76br, 80c, 82c, 94c, 95c, 102c, 103c, 104c, 112c, 135c, 137c, 142c, 146c, 158tr, 158c, 161c, 164br, 198c, 209c, 225tr, 225c, 250c, 251br, 258c, 260c, 261c, 261br, 263c, 272tr, 305tr, 306c

Steven Wooster:
"Reflections on a Tateshina Meadow" for Chelsea Flower Show 2002 by Kay Yamada: 6br

James Young:
19c, 20c, 27br, 51tr, 51c, 58c, 72tr, 88c, 101c, 106c, 130c, 131tr, 131c, 147c, 155c, 159c, 165c, 175c, 178c, 180c, 185c, 203c, 210c, 217c, 229c, 253c, 280c, 284c, 291c, 305c, 306br.

All other images © Dorling Kindersley.

For further information see:
www.dkimages.com

Dorling Kindersley would also like to thank the following:
Helen Fewster, Letitia Luff and Victoria Willan for their editorial assistance; Kathie Gill for the index; and Archie Clapton in Media Resources.